RESOLVE TO LAST

CHOOSE TO FLOURISH

LAURA EVEREST

INDIA · SINGAPORE · MALAYSIA

Notion Press Media Pvt Ltd

No. 50, Chettiyar Agaram Main Road,
Vanagaram, Chennai, Tamil Nadu - 600 095

First Published by Notion Press 2021
Copyright © Laura Everest 2021
All Rights Reserved.

ISBN 978-1-63850-554-9

For Richard, George and Anna: You make my life meaningful in every way.

For my Mother: You taught me never to give up and to always look forward.

For my Father, who inspired me to find my purpose and passion and to recognise the significance of our strengths.

CONTENTS

A BIT ABOUT THE AUTHOR

With more than 30 years of experience, beginning at Harrods, London, where she spent more than a decade, leading and developing large teams, Laura has a successful track record for building talent and elevating business leaders and teams, across diverse professional groups, market sectors and cultures, around the world.

As a Gallup® CliftonStrengths® Coach and Motivational Speaker, Laura highlights where organisations and their people are at their best and focuses on how to develop resilient, authentic leaders and high performing teams through leveraging strengths, with measurable outcomes.

Laura has great energy and injects passion, fun and enthusiasm into every Motivational Keynote and Learning Journey.

Outside of work, Laura is active and sporty, despite the limitations since her accident. With a busy family, 4 large dogs and a cat, you are very likely to find her in her kitchen at the weekends, with music playing, drinking far too much coffee and cooking up a storm for her family and friends!

PRAISE FOR REBUILT TO LAST

We hear about the power of the mind but it's only once in a while we see it in action.

At a time where many people need to be more resilient than ever, this book is amazing. I couldn't put it down.

Passionate, Personal and Powerful.

Laura nails it.

> Phil Bedford, MSC, "The Rebel Networker" #1 Best-selling International Author, Speaker and Entrepreneur

Laura is an exceptional person who has taught me that inner strength, resilience and determination are far more powerful than any pill or stroke of a sugeon's knife.

> Professor Andrew Goldberg OBE MD FRCS (Tr&Orth), Consultant Orthopaedic Surgeon & Visiting Professor of Orthopaedic Surgery, Imperial College London

Many people suffer setbacks; they are unavoidable. Laura teaches us that responding effectively to these is not a factor of genetics but of mindset. Her inspiring story and guidance on approaches to resilience, gives hope and help to everyone. If you only pick up on one of these insights and truly embrace it, you will find yourself in a better place.

Norman Grimes, Managing Director, NG Training

As a Physio for over three decades, motivating injured patients after life changing injury, is one of the challenges of my profession. Laura's absolute diligence towards her rehabilitation and strength of character through so many surgeries and setbacks was and continues to be remarkable.

I learned a lot from working with Laura and the lessons from her book, Rebuilt to Last, are *a must read* whatever your personal challenges in life.

Bev Strathearn, MCSP Senior Physiotherapist

Laura's story is so inspiring. I love her message that resilience is not a "bounce back" but more like a crawl which humanises each of her triumphs along her challenging rebuilding journey. Her writing style is conversational, relatable and packed with nuggets of practical tools and points to ponder of how we can tap into our own strengths to get us through any adversity in life. Thank you Laura!

Nicole Samuels -Williams, Learning & Development Consultant;
Executive Coach

A close friend and colleague of Laura's for a number of years, and even though I know her story well, it was an absolute pleasure and inspiration to read her book, Rebuilt to Last. The difficulties she has had to endure have not stifled Laura's unbounding optimism and ever practical approach to solving problems and rising above and beyond challenges.

Laura not only shares her incredible story, but also provides a great toolkit and brilliant advice for flourishing, which we can all learn from and apply. I highly recommend reading this practical and inspiring book, thank you Laura!

Bev Mileham, Gallup Strengths Coach and
Organisation Culture Consultant

In life's ups and downs, we can all struggle but with real adversity it can often be overwhelming. Laura takes us through her story of how she has been overcoming adversity with a complete account her fight through a lifechanging accident, to show that far from being superhuman, we all have the ability to succeed with determination and resilience.

Nigel Bradford, Owner of NB Consulting

Inspiring!

Laura's book is an inspirational story of her passion, grit and her drive to overcome all the challenges that life has thrown her way! It completely blew me away and provided me with an opportunity for reflection on my own life and the things that I take for granted.

Extremely well written, this book is not only about Laura's struggle to overcome the challenges that life has thrown her way but about staying positive and focusing your energies on what you can achieve and not what you can't.

She has so eloquently shared her story to inspire women (and men) around the world.

Thank you, Laura, for sharing your story.

Zen Kahn, Managing Partner, Zen Professional Development

Laura Everest is a Gallup Certified Strengths Coach

Resilience Defined: the ability to adapt successfully in the face of stress and adversity; to recover from negative emotional experiences, life events, trauma. It relies on our effective responses to environmental challenges and ultimately, our ability to withstand the destructive effects of stress.

INTRODUCTION

I've come to believe that life is one big test.

Often, a series of small challenges that you feel confident in passing, but sometimes, it's like an unexpected exam that you haven't been able to study for; you feel unprepared, anxious and scared of failing. Know that feeling?

I'm sure that you, like me, have experienced times when you feel that the universe is out to get you. It doesn't matter which area of our life that curve ball crashes into, it forces us to face up to situations we'd rather not deal with, but we can't run away from. I don't think I know anyone who hasn't experienced critical points in their life where their resilience and mental toughness have been tested. Do you?

We don't know what challenges will come our way in life, but as I see it, we have two clear choices, either to be crushed, or to develop the strengths to thrive.

Being crushed isn't an option I want to choose, I'm sure you feel the same, but how do we know if we've got what it takes to consistently stay on top? Some people seem to sail through every storm they encounter, whereas others *do* get crushed. How prepared do you feel? I wondered this myself. Over the years, I've read some amazing stories and watched inspirational TED talks of people who have overcome exceptional adversity. Admiration and respect! Achievements way out of my league!

I'm sure you can recall particular figures who stand out for you. Rather like superheroes, their resilience seemed to be on a different level to mine. I assumed they were born with an extraordinary gene that made them tougher and more resistant.

But that was until I had my accident.

Unexpectedly, my life was brought to an abrupt halt and has been completely redefined in ways I would never have imagined.

It's almost impossible to know how you might react in a terrible situation unless you have experience of it but what I have learned, is that you don't need to be a superhero to survive and flourish in life – even when all the chips are stacked against you.

I'm just an average person who is managing to beat all the odds, and I'm thriving despite it all. I'm living proof that you don't need an exceptional gene to flourish, regardless of circumstance. I'm sharing my experience here with you because I've learned that not only can we prepare to get the best out of life, but we actually have far more power than we recognise. You and I have a hidden reserve of strength that we can dig into, which makes us far more capable than we think and I've come to appreciate that we are *so* much stronger than we believe. We can end up doing things that we never thought we could and achieving what we might once have thought was pretty impossible. As with any test, there is a method in preparing, and I can believe I can help you not just to pass, but to be truly successful.

Over the last seven years, I've have felt like a skittle in a bowling alley; challenges have come hurtling at me, repeatedly knocking me over, but I have found a way to stand up again, each time. You may have heard people talking about resilience as "bouncing back". I find that a terrible cliché and actually, rather insulting! You don't *bounce* - unless you've just had a little wobble. Often the difficulties we face can be a tough, ongoing process, that not only takes time but all our determination and effort. Don't you agree? It's rarely about a quick fix.

You and I may face different demons but they challenge us in similar ways. How well do you think you are coping with all the demands placed on you? Do you take care of yourself? Do you have the support you need so that you can cope well with the troubles you face? There is no doubt, every trial and tribulation that comes our way can be a disaster or victory, depending on how we handle it.

Genetics are indeed part of our story, but not all of it, and if those genes weren't naturally bestowed on you, it doesn't matter. Resilience is not just a gift for a select few. You can learn to be resilient. You really can get through *anything* if you want to.

I'm assuming that you've already faced and successfully navigated obstacles in your life. If you think about how you overcame them, you are likely to be more resilient than you think. We all experience 'down' days; let's face it, life is complex. However hard we strive, we have to keep pushing forwards. If you'd like to know how to control your stress, face issues with more certainty and optimism, and be confident that you are well prepared for the future test papers life is preparing for you, I've written this because I believe I can help you. You have the ability to shape your day and your future.

We all have a story to tell.

This is mine.

And this is what I've learned.

THE BEGINNING OF IT ALL

Snapshot of a cherished memory: A long, uninterrupted stretch of pale sandy beach, the Atlantic Ocean on one side, a few scattered palm trees on the other and densely green hills in the distance. This was Sierra Leone, West Africa; a beautiful country which our family was lucky enough to call home for many years, numerous years ago. This was where my love of running began. Nothing, in my opinion, can beat the exhilaration and freedom of running though the surf, with waves breaking next to you, salty spray in the soft air and compact sand under your feet - and nobody around for miles. Nowadays, I believe the beach to be lined with fancy beach bars and hotels. How lucky we were to enjoy it as it was. My Mum used to regularly run the length of the beach and inspired us to do the same. I am truly grateful to her. There have been times in my life where other priorities have taken over but for the last 25 years, running has been a passion, enabling me to disconnect from the world and appreciate the great outdoors. And, of course, it kept me fit. I never visualised it ending quite so abruptly.

Chapter 1
IMPACT

The accident

When I pulled on my running gear at 4:30am I had no idea that this day would change my life in a way that none of us could have imagined.

It was 11th September, *ironically*, a hot, humid morning in Dubai. I could feel the heaviness in the air around me when I set off for my run. I'm an early riser though I can't claim that such an early wake up has ever been fun but once I'm up and out, I rarely regret it.

With 13km completed, I was into the last stretch when I was hit by the car as I was crossing and carried about 30 feet further down the road. Thankfully I remember very little about it (amazing how our brain cleverly protects us in that respect) but I do remember finding myself lying on my back, at the side of the road, with a group of people around me.

I realised immediately that I must have been hit; I'd have no reason to lie there otherwise. I thought that if my head could register this, then my brain must be intact. I slowly tried to move my neck; it felt ok but my back hurt like hell. I was aware that my body was twisted in a very awkward position but I couldn't see much in my line of vision (I was cautious not to move my head too much). I scanned down my body to my feet. My right foot was hanging off, the toe of my trainer touching the tarmac preventing my foot separating from my leg completely, the broken bones in my lower leg protruding clearly, like someone sticking up two fingers. My left foot was positioned at an impossible angle, the bone protruding at the side.

People were talking around me and I could hear panic and urgency in their voices. They kept saying to me *"stay with us"*. I wondered where they thought I was planning to go. It occurred to me that they thought I might die. I put the question to myself: *Is this it?* It took me just a few seconds to elect life over death - I absolutely was *not* ready to die! With a young family, work that I loved and so much I still wanted to achieve in life, it definitely wasn't my time! I decided there and then that whatever the damage, there would be people who could fix me.

No one can possibly guess how they might react in such a situation but my mind moved immediately into action mode and my focus turned to what needed to be done. Pain was secondary; I seemed to be able to disconnect from it for the most part. The will to live was overriding. My husband, Richard, needed to be contacted; my office needed to get someone to replace me in the training room that morning; I needed medical help. There was an amazing Indian lady by my side, trying to keep everyone calm and support me until the ambulance arrived (I don't know her name and have been unable to contact her - but if it happens to be you who is reading this, I will never be able to thank you enough!).

I endeavoured to keep my right foot elevated – first aid training kicking in (pardon the pun). Keeping the toe of my trainer in contact with the road, I was trying not to disengage my foot entirely. It wasn't easy. Weirdly, I felt quite calm – shock, probably. I recognised one of the guys standing around me – I'm pretty good with faces. I had worked with him somewhere but when I commented on it to him, he looked utterly horrified to be singled out and was quite certain that he didn't know me.

Later I realised that with all the cuts and wounds, I had probably looked pretty unrecognisable.

I must have swung in and out of consciousness, thereafter, because I don't remember the ambulance arriving but I have memory flashes of being tended to very efficiently. Richard arrived as I was being moved into the ambulance. I'm very glad he was spared the scene beforehand. When I arrived at the hospital, it was all stations go. I had around 10 medical staff working on me at the same time. My clothes were cut off, so too, was my wedding ring. My fingers had swollen like blown up rubber gloves. There was much to be done to stabilise me before the scans and X -rays could commence. My right foot was hastily sewn back on. My left foot was facing in the opposite direction and had lost pulse. This posed a big concern and my foot was urgently forced back into place. Alcohol was poured over my left arm, much of the lower half, from my elbow to my wrist, seemed to be missing. I'm not going to pretend; it was an excruciating process but the medical team were excellent and they got me through it as quickly as they could.

The damage

Scans and X-rays revealed that there was more damage than I had initially thought. Apart from the dreadful injury to my right ankle, my left ankle was completely crushed. I had separated my left hamstring (the area where the car had first made contact), I had broken my left elbow and half of my lower arm was missing. My right wrist was dislocated, as were all my fingers. I had fractured ribs and my whole back had gone into spasm. As you might imagine, running clothes don't exactly offer you much protection from being rolled over tarmac, so I had plenty of surface damage. Not a very pretty sight. With unbelievable luck, however, I had no serious damage to my head or spine and had not ruptured any vital organs. Silver linings!

A little bit of humour

Preparing for surgery, there was a small hiccup when the team tried to remove my nail polish and mortified, I had to explain that it was a 'Gellish' varnish which didn't come off without specialist solution! Richard was asked to phone the salon and like a scene from a comedy, he tried relaying instructions to the ER team on how to remove the polish! Honestly, it was a bizarre situation but it provided a bit of light relief at an otherwise serious time. Unbelievably, the polish was stubborn (well worth the cost!) and in the end it was decided that getting me to Theatre was more important than wasting time trying to remove it.

My reality

My injuries were plentiful, I faced hours of surgery and there were so many unknowns facing me. Was I concerned? Of course. Courage is not an absence of fear but I realised that panicking wouldn't serve any useful purpose and I had to accept that the challenge in front of me wouldn't wait or disappear; that the sooner we got on with the surgery, the better. My only hope was to place my trust in the people who could help me. I deliberately didn't allow my thinking to wander down the *'what if?'* route. I made up my mind that I would be ok and just focused on the immediate solutions in front of me.

Post theatre

When I came round from the initial 9 hours of surgery, there were several surgeons and nursing staff standing by my bed. They told me that I was very lucky to be alive and that I needed to be aware of the severity of my injuries. They had managed to fix my feet back on, though there was clearly doubt that I would walk again.

My left arm was an ongoing discussion point because the surgeons were still deciding how to begin to repair it. I was taken back to Theatre and they had another go. I returned with what looked like cling film wrapped around it and a pump to remove fluid. It wasn't a pretty sight and I wasn't surprised that one of my friends threw up when he saw it. The surgeons felt I would ultimately need several skin grafts to repair it and there was concern that I might never be able to straighten my arm.

It must have been a terrible shock for my family and I worried for my kids, George and Anna. Richard decided to bring them into Intensive Care, to see me that first night, after my surgery, because he felt it was better for them to see and speak with me, than to imagine the unknown worst, at home. Although I resembled something from a comic movie, swathed in bandages from head to toe, and only just conscious, I was determined that they would know that I would be ok.

Taking back control

The big picture was pretty overwhelming and dismal. But what the doctors visualised for me, compared to what I knew about myself, were very different perspectives. I knew that if I could focus my mind on what I needed to do I would get through it somehow.

Here's what I tell myself to keep my anxiety in check: *Stay in the present; don't over analyse; accept there is only so much that can be done at a time and don't get overwhelmed in detail.* Sometimes it can sound like a mantra but it helps me every time I feel challenged.

If you find that you feel stressed and overwhelmed at times, I can't emphasise enough how important it is to be able feel in control of your environment, when you can't control anything else. In this respect, I resonate strongly with the concept that Stephen Covey articulates in his book, *The 7 Habits of Highly Effective People*, relating to our *Circle of Concern* and our *Circle of Influence (Diagram below)* where he encourages us to question how we anticipate problems and explains how we can proactively focus our efforts and influence the outcomes we want to see.

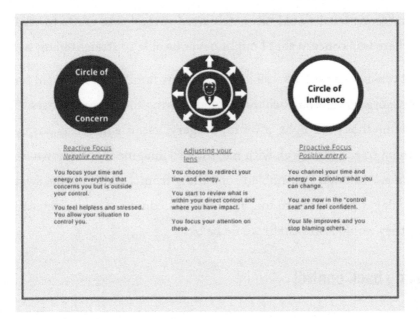

To explain it simply:

- Your *Circle of Concern* includes the wide range of worries you have in the world, your work and life – including health, family, finances, the economy, the Covid pandemic etc. Everything you include inside this circle, is a concern and matters to you.

- Your *Circle of Influence* are the things that concern you but which you *can do something about*; changing things that are within your control and where you can create impact. You have more power than you think over situations that seem out of your control.

I am a great believer that there is no point in wasting energy over things you can't change. I wanted to get better and it was therefore essential that I put myself in the control seat, so I could manage my own recovery as far as possible. To do this, I reviewed each of my injuries separately and decided what I could do to influence the recovery of each one. I had an action plan! The first thing was managing the pain. My back, the least serious of my injuries, was not only the most painful but the most debilitating and I knew that I couldn't really move very much until I got that pain under better control. I started with a Tens machine (an electric nerve stimulator which gently pulses through the skin and helps relieve pain) and light massage. I took all my pain at face value – at no point did I allow my mind to picture the broken bones and tissue. It wouldn't serve a helpful purpose.

I like to pretend that when I heard the word "bedpan" I was out of bed faster than anyone could imagine possible! That's not far from truth; following the surgeons' advice, inch by inch, using my right wrist (less painful) I practiced moving until I could indeed slowly negotiate my way into, and out of, a wheelchair. Was it frustrating? Yes. Did I feel sorry for myself? Yes. Did it hurt? Terribly. But what mattered more to me was getting better.

Fact vs emotion

Emotions play an important role in how we think and behave. They give us information about what we're experiencing and help us know how to react. Our responses result from the way in which we appraise our situation. It's important to identify what we are feeling, label that emotion to clearly understand what it is telling us, so that we can figure out the most helpful way to respond to it. Putting feelings into words can help us process them better and gives us more power over them. (*I will share more about this in due course*). Emotions are a powerful guide but they can derail us if we allow them to; it is easy to become trapped behind our own emotional defences. As you have probably experienced, pain can play havoc with your emotions. I learned very quickly not to try and reason with emotions but to separate *fact* and *emotion,* in the process more clearly focus on the facts and organise an action plan that kept me on track with building my own recovery.

Striving for some normality

A week after I came out of the High Dependency ward, a colleague from my company rang me to ask if I would like a project to work on. You may think me crazy but it was the lifeline I needed to keep my mind connecting to normality. It's so easy to succumb to feeling like a victim but then it becomes harder to get out of that negative thinking zone. Of course, I could only manage very small amounts of work at a time. Pain could be overwhelming; it fogged my mind and I was easily exhausted. But every little bit I did, made me feel more in control and, with time, I could manage to do more.

The hospital was far from glamorous but the nursing staff were excellent. Richard, the children and my Besties, visited me every day and so many other friends and work colleagues that came too. I was truly grateful to them all. Amazingly, after only 12 days in hospital, I was allowed to go home.

Richard, not used to seeing me so vulnerable, found it difficult to connect emotionally but, practical as ever, he built a series of ramps inside and outside the villa, for my wheelchair. He and the children had made me a wonderful temporary bedroom downstairs, so that I could be as comfortable as possible and be at the centre of family life. Our son, George, just 13 years old, reacted to my accident by developing terrible stomach pain and was sick for a few days. Thereafter, he did everything he could think of, to help look after me. Our daughter, Anna, only 10 years old, was a little withdrawn but was mostly as sweet and good as little girls are. As a quiet child, we thought all was ok but in fact it proved to be a concern further down the line.

Establishing routines

My parents, obviously horrified to hear of my situation, dropped everything and came out to Dubai to help look after me and our family. They arrived from UK the day after I returned home and soon, we all settled into a routine. For the 6 months that they ended up staying to help us, they were incredible; we wouldn't have been able to manage as we did, without them. It was important to me that our children's routine was interrupted as little as possible and, with my parents' help, things quickly settled down. Although at first, I was still enveloped in bandages and mostly bed bound, I insisted on going into the kitchen every day, in my wheelchair, to help where I could prepare school packed lunches and meals for the day. As a keen cook, I couldn't wait to get back to my regular routine of cooking and baking. As often as pain would allow, I would join everyone for dinner in the evening. I really wanted to feel normal. As I became stronger, I was able to add more activities into my day, including work, physio and exercise.

Have you noticed when you are unwell, that despite your best efforts, everything around you seems to happen at a super-fast pace? I wanted to keep up. I have always been so full of energy, so used to being busy, and it was really frustrating not to be able to do all the things I wanted to do. Patience, unfortunately, is not one of my virtues. I think you'll agree that there are times we need to press our 'reset' button. We can put immense pressure on ourselves to try and do everything. I recognise that sometimes I can be my own worst enemy in this respect. When you feel overwhelmed, are you good at cutting back less important things? I find it hard to say 'No' and put myself first. Maybe you do too. How do you set boundaries?

What I found very helpful was to create a new daily routine for myself, prioritising what was really important and what wasn't and developing some simple actions to help me feel organised and in control once more. It provided a very necessary structure for me to focus on healthier coping mechanisms. Consistency matters. As Aristotle says: *"We are what we repeatedly do. Excellence then, is not an act, but a habit."*

Being organised, focused and getting stuff done, are key strengths of mine, so establishing a planned structure to my days automatically motivated me. Starting small and adding more tasks over time, I had clarity, direction and focal points to work towards. I felt energised and ticking off my daily achievements gave me a positive lift. I really feel that this fast tracked my recovery.

Working to our strengths is important and so is prioritising self-care. If you thrive on schedules and have a solid daily routine, I don't need to tell you how helpful a routine can be for our wellbeing, particularly in times of unpredictability, uncertainty and stress.

Back to hospital

After five weeks at home, my first round of stitches needed to be removed. With almost one hundred stitches spread between my ankles, arm and head, it wasn't a five-minute job, nor was it a comfortable one. Whilst being checked over, it became evident that I needed further surgery on my left thigh; the area which made initial contact with the car. My hamstring had been permanently separated but a large hematoma had formed in the area and needed swift attention.

This time, a different hospital, another surgeon and an alternative method. Having had a vast amount of anaesthesia in such a short time, the surgeon suggested this operation could be performed under local, as opposed to general, anaesthetic. Feeling overly brave following the removal of so many stitches, I agreed. Well, it was honestly *horrendously* painful, despite many injections to numb the area and the surgeon said afterwards how incredibly courageous I was! That was the first and last time I will choose to follow that route. From this day forwards, my motto is: *Put me under and let me sleep through it!* One needs to have courage but there is no point setting up extra hurdles to jump over when you don't need to. Pick your battles!

Recovery

For the first few weeks, with both arms bound and fragile, I wasn't physically able to wheel myself in the wheelchair, so everyone took turns to push me in it. I was able to sit upright on the bed, during the day, as much as my back pain would allow; at night I lay on my back, with each of my heavily bandaged legs supported on pillows and each of my arms, too. Most nights my body screamed out from the strain of being stuck in one position but I was unable to shift much more than an inch or so. Each small twist of movement caused sharp pain in my back, which radiated down my legs and up through my shoulders, into my neck. If I flinched with the sudden tensing pain, it triggered a domino effect; every part of my body tightening and contracting. Intense, debilitating pain. The answer was to move as little as possible. I found I could manage the pain but sleep wasn't easy. Music helped distract me, so I'd spend the small hours listening to playlist after playlist, trying not to watch the clock, waiting for the darkness to break into the new day. Sometimes I cried with frustration but, overall, I gritted my teeth and got through it. During the night, I would phone Richard, or our lovely Housekeeper, if I needed to use the loo. I also needed help to shower and clean my teeth. I did not enjoy feeling so vulnerable, I've always been so capable and independent but I had to accept there were things outside my control and I learned, very soon, to be grateful for all the people helping and supporting me. No one wants to be around a misery, so I made a huge effort to focus on what was going right, rather than what was wrong.

Celebrating the victories

How easily can you call to mind your achievements, those things you are most proud of? We have an innate ability to focus on disasters first, so the chances are you may instinctively recall what hasn't worked, rather than what has, and even more so when you are going through tough times, when it becomes harder to see beyond those things that challenge you. A Victory List - another concept from Stephen Covey, is about noting down all your accomplishments in a day - simple things that are challenging and important at the time and it is a great way to help you prioritise, focus and celebrate your accomplishments.

I made my Victory List (and I still use them all the time). Every little thing that I achieved, went on that list - moving my arm a quarter of an inch, being able to sit in the wheelchair all the way through dinner with the family...Tiny wins maybe, but they soon mounted up and I was able to see just how far I had come, how much I was achieving, and that alone was so motivating, especially at times when I felt discouraged that my recovery was taking forever. I know that you must have challenges of your own to get through. Might keeping a Victory List help you to recognise your achievements and celebrate your wins?

Building Strength

Are sport and exercise a regular part of your life? Do you look forward to working out, or does the thought of a daily exercise programme fill you with horror?

We are always being told about the benefits of exercise for boosting our health and wellbeing and there is overwhelming evidence in its favour. Research convincingly proves that people who lead active lifestyles are less likely to suffer from physical and mental illness and are more likely to live longer. And even better, the chemicals released in our brain (endorphins) when we exercise, lift our mood and can reduce pain. Forgive me if I'm preaching to the converted but if exercise isn't your thing, *please* reconsider. You don't have to become an Olympian athlete to boost your energy and endurance. I believe that just about everybody can find a physical activity that they enjoy.

Being active is a fundamental part of my life. In fact, the surgeons informed me that if I hadn't been so physically fit before my accident, I probably wouldn't have survived. One of the most difficult outcomes from my accident is that I can never run or do impact sport again. I still struggle to find my peace with it, even though I'm so grateful that I can do so many other things.

Despite the extensive damage to my limbs and back, I was determined to rebuild my physical strength. My ankles were the biggest concern since I was not allowed to put any weight on them whatsoever. I developed an innovative range of exercises which wouldn't compromise my ankles. Working out was not a chore for me and it became part of my morning routine once again. I challenged myself every day to beat my last "Personal Best" and after a few weeks, I was using hand weights, doing half press-ups, sit ups and kneeling squats. I could see muscle returning. It felt good. I felt rejuvenated! My family watched my creative endeavours with fascination. I know they didn't understand my motivation but it pleased me enormously to feel I was achieving something. Highly energized and always on the move, the hardest thing *by far*, for me, was being confined to a wheelchair. I *hated* the inaction. I *hated* that I couldn't get about. I *hated* being stuck indoors.

To distract my negative thoughts, I focused on my *Circle of Influence* and found great comfort in work. I had been handed a project to organise a team training event for 80 high flying merchandisers. There were many different aspects to cover and my client had an ambitious vision of what he wanted it to be. It proved quite complex to bring together but it played to my strengths. My client and colleagues joined me for meetings, sitting around my bedside. Not only did I enjoy the whole process of orchestrating the event, I facilitated that training programme, in my wheelchair, 11 weeks after the accident. It was a great success for my client and a personal win for me.

I had a fantastic physiotherapist, Bev Strathearn. Open and direct, she took one look at my feet and pulled no punches in telling me that I was facing a major challenge to get back up on my feet again. She fixed the pain in my back with acupuncture and worked with me slowly but surely, motivating me to achieve each of our goals and setting my perspective to rights each time I was knocked back. Bev was tough but I know she'll agree that I was a very good student; she was my godsend for years.

Resolve and innovation!

"Being challenged in life is inevitable; being defeated is optional". Roger Crawford

The first time we went out was a challenge and a victory. One weekend, I had, like a small child, thrown a tantrum and insisted that I was taken out for lunch. Still wrapped up in bandages, the family reacted with trepidation but I was absolutely determined! I felt claustrophobic being confined to the villa. I needed to be part of a different environment. The family understood. Where there's a will, there's a way! I was able to leverage myself out of the wheelchair and holding the bar inside the door of a taxi (our Landcruiser was too high to manage this at that time), I could swing myself onto the backseat, without my ankles being compromised in any way. Exhausting effort maybe but it was so liberating to get out. Soon this method of travelling became a regular way for me to get about. There was one awful time, when getting into a taxi to leave a venue, there was a snap, the handle came off in my hand and I fell, backside first onto the road, but generally, it was a great option. Soon after, with my Mum accompanying me (bathroom assistance!), I was able to get back into the training room once more.

As I became stronger, we decided it was time to figure out a way for me to get into the back of my Landcruiser, rather than keep relying on taxis. The key issue was the height. My family were innovative and I was strong. Richard tied TRX straps inside the very back of the Landcruiser. My Mum had purchased a large, firm majalis cushion which raised my wheelchair seat by several inches. I was able to lift myself out of the wheelchair using just my upper body and pull myself into the boot of the car, using those TRX straps, without putting any weight onto my legs or feet. It looked like a circus act but it became a slick one pretty quickly.

A "Person of Determination"

As a "Person of Determination" in Dubai, there are many initiatives the government have taken in the latter years, to address the needs of the disabled. At the beginning of my journey these were yet to be put in place and I soon realised how difficult it actually was, to be a disabled person. If you have had reason to use a disabled washroom you may have noticed that most hand basins, mirrors and towels are set at a non-disabled height; loos are squished in the corner, making them tricky to negotiate when in a wheelchair. Many hotels and offices, including my own, had ramps at their entrance but once inside, there were limited options to get about. I have been to hotels where 4 strong staff, at a time, have carried me in my wheelchair up and down steps! I am very grateful that the recent initiatives have now made all of this so much easier for every person of determination. It's led me to appreciate things I had taken for granted.

Chapter 2
MINDSET MATTERS

The second knock

After 12 weeks in the wheelchair, I was desperate to get out of it and eagerly awaited my appointment with the Trauma Surgeon. My parents took me to the hospital. I was feeling optimistic and chatted happily to the medical staff, in anticipation, as I went through the process of having further X-rays and checks. The results showed that my damaged arms and hands were repairing well, as was my back (the pain was much reduced). All my cuts and scrapes were healing to the doctor's satisfaction. But my aspirations of getting out of that wheelchair were utterly crushed when the Surgeon advised me gravely, that my ankles were still far from recovery. He said they were the worst injuries he had seen and that I needed to remain off my feet for several more weeks. I was devastated! It felt like I was back to Square One! I cried all the way home. I was inconsolable all day and brooded over my misfortune for most of the night. I relived my accident all over again in my mind. I felt angry that the car had hit me. I felt that the universe was conspiring against me and that despite all my effort and positivity, nothing was improving. As a Catholic, I was convinced God wasn't helping me either and I raged at Him, too. I was bitter and wretched and full of pity for myself. I hated being so broken, feeling so vulnerable, needing so much help. I wanted to be independent, to get back to my life as it had been but, instead, I felt completely dependent on everyone around me. Everybody was being so kind and I knew I was being unreasonable – but I HATED being in that wheelchair. And I hated myself for feeling so diminished.

I'm sure, like me, you have experienced first-hand, that life is not always kind or fair. But, at the end of the day, it is what it is. It's very easy when you're unhappy to play the blame game and place the responsibility of your misfortune on other people, or on unfair situations, but it's a hopeless cycle. As much as I felt sorry for myself, I recognised that sitting in victim zone, wasn't going to get me anywhere. The longer my mind dwelled on the things that were upsetting me, the more helpless I felt and, fortunately, or unfortunately, I like to feel in control! There is no doubt that when you stop focusing on the problem, you create the headspace to think of viable solutions. By the morning, I had made up my mind to refocus on my *Circle of Influence* and devise a plan. I needed a focus and goals to achieve, a purpose. My family were relieved to see I was my positive self once more and were as supportive as ever.

I had three key actions:

1. Get fit physically. Essential to helping me to become stronger, more independent and manage more things for myself.

2. Get fit mentally. To ensure I was on top of our business training objectives, up to date with current information and new ideas and to work on new leadership training programmes, which would ensure that I would be back with full confidence in my role as a Leadership Training Consultant.

3. Spend "quality" time in the kitchen. Cooking, baking, ice cream making, tempering chocolate...and I'm in a happy place. It's a

passion, a comfort, a de-stressor and a time for quiet reflection and contemplation, as I work.

I set a goal for every day and actions to achieve them. This included physio with Bev and stamina weight training (all designed for no impact on my ankles). I began immediately. After three weeks of consistent effort I returned to work, despite the limitations of being in the wheelchair with arms and legs still bandaged, with everyone's support, I was set up for success. Moreover, with our fridge and every friend's freezer filled with delicious offerings, I was feeling happy, more relaxed and confident.

None of us choose to feel overwhelmed, stuck, or thwarted, but taking responsibility to regain ownership of your life is crucial for moving forwards. One of my favourite quotes is: *Life isn't about waiting for the storm to pass; it's about learning to dance in the rain.* Well, one of the key things I have learned from this challenging time is that I might not be able to control what adversity I have to face, but my life feels considerably better when I can find a way to manage those challenging situations to my advantage. And with that quote in mind, I'm practising every damned dance there is! When you find your best self, you can achieve remarkable things. How well do you take responsibility for your life when the chips are stacked against you?

Nearly 8 weeks later, feeling very tense, we returned to the hospital for more X-rays and scans. This time, I was given the all-clear to start getting back on my feet. *Ohhh...the relief!* The *joy* that I could start getting my life back on track! I was so grateful not to be confined to that chair any longer. If I could've got up then and there, I would have danced a little jig!

My heart goes out to you if you are wheelchair or bed bound. You have strength of character that I don't possess! I applaud you.

We returned home from the hospital via *'Life Pharmacy'*. If you happen to live in Dubai you will know that it sells a multitude of healthcare products, including crutches. I came home armed and ready to get started.

Getting back up with perseverance and belief

"You never know how strong you are until being strong is your only choice". Bob Marley

I had anticipated that it wouldn't be easy to just get out of the wheelchair and start walking and I wasn't wrong. But I was determined. Two of my top Gallup® CliftonStrengths® are Achiever® and Focus® and I leveraged the hell out of them! My body was uncoordinated and wobbly. My back hurt and my arms screamed out in pain when I supported myself on crutches. My ankles were mostly numb, so it was difficult to stand, let alone try to walk. With my Mum and Richard helping me to balance, my Dad standing behind me with the wheelchair almost under my knees, in case I fell, and my children holding their breath, I started taking my first steps. It hurt, it felt peculiar and each step required my full concentration but I was elated. Of course, I could only manage a few steps but that was the just the first day. The next day, my pain and coordination were no better but I persevered. Every day, I worked harder and longer until I was managing to get about with the crutches as support, slowly but surely. The pain was tough to take, especially during the night. Payback for pushing my body so hard. But as they say: *no pain, no gain*. I had no intention of backing down. I leaned into my innate toolkit of strengths and I soldiered on.

You may be familiar with the term *'Grit'*. Angela Duckworth is an expert on this subject. Grit is described as the passion and perseverance to achieve long term goals. I found I had grit but just like our strengths, it takes practice to develop and grow. Being *gritty* is not about being more courageous, more talented, or intelligent than anyone else, it's about being consistent, dedicated to keep practicing and believing that you can.

"If you are going to win any battle, you have to do one thing: You have to make the mind run the body. Never let the body tell the mind what to do. The body is never tired if the mind is not tired"- General George S Patten Junior. I know this to be true. I have trained leaders on the importance of mindset for years but until I retaught myself how to walk, I hadn't truly appreciated what we are capable of if we want to achieve something badly enough.

It took me hours of practice every day but six weeks later, when I returned for my check up with the surgeon, he was utterly amazed when I walked steadily, with my new crutches, into his office. I learned then that he and the other surgeons doubted that it would be possible for me to walk again. They felt my injuries were too great. All I can say is that I'm very glad they didn't share their opinion with me on my last visit. Our beliefs can put boundaries and limitations on what we perceive to be possible. Failure scares us and that prevents us from taking chances. Without feeling confined by the surgeons' perceptions, I had no self-limiting beliefs – it never occurred to me that I might not get up and walk and so I got on with trying, believing that I could.

Science proves **that if you have a mindset that is always looking for success and improvement, you'll find it,** so if you truly believe you *can* do something, the odds are that you probably can. This doesn't mean that you believe you *can't* fail in your endeavours but it reduces your *fear* of failure, giving you the confidence to attempt it. Belief is a powerful motivator, driving us to persevere. As Gandhi observed: *"Men often become* *what they believe themselves to be. If I believe I cannot do something, it makes me incapable of doing it. But when I believe I can, then I acquire the ability to do it even if I didn't have it in the beginning".*

Most of us underestimate what we are capable of. We rarely give ourselves enough credit. Your self-belief will determine how well you access your strengths and realise your true potential. If you trust in your abilities, know your strengths and what you are capable of, it gives you the confidence to try new things, to stand up for yourself, say *'yes'*, aim high, and have the self-assurance that you are making the right decisions. It opens you up to seeing new possibilities, to make the changes you want to see in your life.

You can never grow to become your best self unless you *believe* you can, so don't allow self-limiting thoughts to sabotage your progress. Belief drives what you do and determines what you will achieve.

Challenging situations will always put pressure on our mental toughness. What beliefs and expectations do you have of yourself? Do they serve to build your confidence, or undermine who you could become? Are you accomplishing the things you value? How do you manage those negative thoughts which strive to undermine you?

Through the setbacks I have faced, I have come to recognise the value of effort, perseverance and challenging myself. I refuse to accept defeat by default, to give up without at least trying. Without believing in myself, I would never have left the confines of that wretched wheelchair. Mindset matters. I still have a mountain of issues to overcome and you may, too, but when you take control of your mindset, who knows how far you can go?

A point for reflection: *We become what we think about.*

A question for consideration: *How do your thoughts influence your experiences in life?*

Resilient responses: *For strategies on developing a healthy mindset to get you through the tough times, please see* **Toolkit for Flourishing: Mindset Matters; Taking Control**

Chapter 3
DÉJÀ VU

A Rollercoaster

Naively I had hoped that once I was up and walking, my life would be back on track and uninterrupted by any more hospital check-ups.

My less serious injuries had healed well - even my left arm, though terribly scarred, was fixing itself without, unbelievably, the need for skin grafts. Unfortunately, my ankles were still a big problem. Fixed with a copious number of pins and plates and resembling Meccano structures, the metal work was restricting my movement and causing pain and the bones were re-healing awkwardly. Both my ankles needed further surgical attention – the left one, particularly.

I was in and out of hospital whilst new pins were added, some were removed and my ankle bones were recut. Back in the wheelchair, I was desperate, despite the constant pain, to get back on my feet and escape feeling so dependent and so helpless. As soon as I physically could, I was up on my crutches and learning to walk again. I seemed to be stuck in this endless pattern. I developed tendonitis in my shoulder from the strain of relying so heavily on crutches. In between my surgeries, I tried to build stamina, slowly walking along the beach track, gradually improving my distance and speed. A key highlight was being able to get back on our much-loved boat. I love being on the water – and whilst I wasn't able to swim, or get my feet and arm wet, the sheer enjoyment of being outdoors, enjoying the sea air, was exhilarating.

Exactly one year to the date of my accident, I was back in hospital having my ninth operation. The surgeon termed it as *"massive invasive surgery"* and I can't say that the thought of this was particularly comforting but I accepted that I needed the procedure to be done. This time I had an epidural to help with pain relief. My experience was awful. Would you believe I had a terrible reaction to it?! I felt seriously spaced out – scarily dizzy with a terrible headache. I came out in a rash all over. Honestly, I was frightened to close my eyes and sleep, in case I wouldn't wake up ever again. Have you ever had an epidural? What was your experience of it? Hopefully, better than mine. The anaesthetist said in all the many years he had been working, I was only the second person in whom he had seen such an adverse reaction! He carried out a spinal tap and thankfully, monitored me very closely. My Birthday also happened to coincide with my surgery. What a day! The nursing staff tried so hard to make me feel better- they blew up surgical gloves, like balloons, with funny faces drawn onto them and even bought me a cake. I felt so ill that it was difficult to feel enthusiastic but I really appreciated their kindness. Whilst the epidural did indeed block the pain in my leg, I have to say that I found the lack of sensation made it harder for me to move around (and maybe that was the point!) so after that experience, I decided no more epidurals for me, moving forwards!

I think it's fair to say that, over the years, I have become quite an expert in the field of hospitals, operating theatres and the processes involved in surgical procedures. It has occurred to me that whilst there are lucky people (maybe you are one of them?) who get to critique hotels, spas and restaurants, perhaps this might be a new, less glamorous opportunity for me. Knowing my journey is an ongoing one, with many more surgeries ahead, I'm beginning to wonder if this will turn into a lucrative role in time to come! Watch this space...

Nine surgeries, twelve months; my life and wellbeing during this year was a rollercoaster of highs and lows, both mentally and physically, as I dipped to a low point after each surgery, slowly picking myself up, redirecting my focus and working my way back to fitness, fun and work, only to repeat this process, over and over and over. It felt like *Groundhog Day*, stuck in a repetitive time loop and finding it difficult to move forwards but desperately recording each little win, so that I could see that I was making progress.

New experiences

At the end of the year, I travelled to Johannesburg to work with one of my favourite pharma clients. I was in a new cast, on crutches, and I couldn't manage the stairs to the aircraft. It was my first experience of entering the plane by the 'back door' - wheelchair access. Levied up on a raised platform, I wondered at first if I was going to be placed in the Hold, strapped in next to the luggage. Very relieved to find that wasn't the case, though being the very last passenger on the tarmac, I provided on-board entertainment for the rest of my fellow travellers on the plane. I have now become a dab hand at travelling this way – and use to being the star attraction on entering the aircraft!

Three weeks after my work trip, Richard, the children and I flew out to Sri Lanka to celebrate a milestone Birthday for my best friend, Biddi, and her family (also my close friends), Mandi and Bonita. The funniest thing occurred when we arrived at Colombo International airport. For some bizarre reason, they were all convinced that I was Princess Diana! I tried to explain, firstly, that I wasn't, and secondly, that Princess Diana had very unfortunately passed away several years beforehand but, as you can imagine, communication was a little restricted due to our differences in language. With a Special Assistant pushing my wheelchair, we were whizzed through customs, with the utmost care and service. I can't pretend that the experience wasn't a good one and it did make us all giggle!

Dips and peaks

Having ended the year on a holiday high, the new year began with more surgery. Another dip. By February I had had three more operations. My surgeon was also trying to inject heavy doses of cortisone into my left ankle to relieve the pain. It was a careful decision because as much as the cortisone would help, the side effect is bone deterioration – and hot flushes! It was a risk worth taking because despite the adverse reactions, it gave me the pain relief which we had hoped for.

There is no doubt that the more operations I had, the more mundane they became. I would take a taxi to the hospital, sometimes straight from work meetings, work on my laptop until time for the surgery, then dressed for the starring role, I would be taken to Theatre ready for "showtime".

I have learned to manage the pain and cope with the many frustrations because I enjoy my work, I love to be joyful and social and I want to relish all the things that matter to me. I cannot deny, however, that having one surgery after the next wasn't exhausting; one step forwards, two steps back – a bit like dancing, except this wasn't fun, and it wasn't ultimately fixing the problem with my ankles.

I have learned to be highly confident on crutches and I can walk on them faster than some people can jog. However, trying to carry training materials and a laptop whilst on crutches, is always challenging, and becomes even more so, when I travel overseas to work. The metal in my legs generally set off every security alarm and in some countries that has caused concern! I always carry photos of my X-rays everywhere I go (it saves so much time explaining!) being body searched is now par for the course at every airport, as well as having my cast and crutches well and truly examined.

One of my strengths is positivity; I find it ironic that my Blood group is B+.

April brought with it a double celebration which lifted us all. The first, Richard's milestone Birthday. We decided to hold a big party. We flew my parents out to join us and had a fabulous time. Dodgy feet or not, I even danced - I love to dance – and it was worth every bit of the pain afterwards! Two weeks later it was our 25th Wedding Anniversary and Richard and I flew to Santorini – can you believe, our first ever holiday without George and Anna?! It was gorgeous, we enjoyed every minute of it.

I have a particular passion for Greece. We, as a family, along with my Parents, my Brother and Sister-in-Law, Graham and Lucy, and their 3 lovely children, have spent a few summers together, in Crete. The mountains... the sea...the olive groves...all in one snapshot. A perfect eyeful. Especially in the early morning. Aside from running on the beaches in Africa, this was my favourite place to run. Graham, Richard and I would get up extra early to take advantage of the cool mornings and often my Mum and George would join us, too. Obviously, my accident put a stop to running but it didn't stop me walking, albeit with the support of crutches and ankle splints. I'm so grateful to have these very happy memories during this otherwise testing time.

By the end of the second year, I had racked up a total of twelve major surgeries, the maximum number of cortisone injections, vast quantities of anaesthetic and medication and had completed relentless rounds of physiotherapy. My trusty crutches had snapped from overuse and I felt quite bereft to be replacing them. Despite everyone's best efforts, it became increasingly evident that I needed further expert help and our thoughts turned to ankle replacement surgery.

It took a few months of research and emails to finally meet the brilliant Mr Andrew Goldberg, in London. If any of you have an ankle problem – Mr G's your guy! The first thing I thought when I met him was that he was too young to be so eminent. He thought I looked too young, too (well, certainly younger than most of his patients, going through the same thing). It made me laugh. I knew we'd get along and since that time, I know him to be a remarkably good man and a brilliant surgeon.

Having studied my X-rays he recognised that both my ankles needed attention but with the hardware and software in my left ankle completely damaged, we decided that needed immediate focus. We discussed fusion and ankle replacement and ultimately decided that ankle replacement was my immediate route forward. Rather than feeling anxious about the procedure, I felt a new wave of positivity and optimism – and awe at what can be done courtesy of modern medicine!

People have asked me if I become more resilient, with each setback. Honestly, the answer is 'no' and 'yes'. Getting past each hurdle is a mental game. You have to be determined and you have to persevere. Most of us have a tendency to underestimate ourselves and our capabilities. And tough times, whether we like it or not, forces us to respond in ways beyond what we thought was possible.

When we initially face a difficult situation, we instinctively see it as a threat to our wellbeing and the emotions that surface in response, pull us down into a miserable place where we'd rather not be. We feel vulnerable and outside our sphere of control. It takes effort to refocus our mind on solutions and positive outcomes. However, what I now know for sure, is that if you keep practicing the right strategies and leverage your personal strengths, you definitely rise more quickly.

What really helps is to know the outcome you want to see. Why does it matter to you? No one becomes successful because they find an easy path but when you know what you want and why, you find a way to overcome those obstacles and keep going. Visualise that outcome. Believe it. Then summon up all your personal resources to help you find a way through. As I've mentioned before, I have an aversion to the term *"bounce back"* simply because when managing adversity, rarely do we *"bounce"*, rather, it's a process to recovery and learning how to thrive.

If you want to ace the tests that life throws at you, you have to endure all the challenges, review your successes, recognise where you are strong, what holds you back and then focus everything you've got, on where you want to be.

As the late, great Maya Angelou said *"It is necessary to encounter the defeats, so you can know who you are, what you can rise from, how you can still come out of it."*

A point for reflection: *Your setbacks do not define your future.*

A question for consideration: *How do you explain your setbacks to yourself?*

Resilient responses: *For strategies on countering life's pitfall, please see:* **Toolkit for Flourishing: A Glass Half Full**

Chapter 4
A JUGGLING ACT

It was fast approaching three years since my accident and now, in the run up to the ankle replacement surgery, we had another major setback at home.

Our sweet daughter was experiencing personal trauma of her own which majorly compromised her values, behaviour and our family unit. It was bewildering for Anna herself, and a deeply distressing time for us all. We felt completely out of our depth and Richard and I worried endlessly because we didn't know who to turn to, to help us. As parents, we questioned ourselves first. *"What did we miss?"*. *"Should we have done something differently?"*. In the absence of information, it's very easy to fall back into familiar habits of negative thinking and fill the gaps in knowledge by catastrophising the situation. I tend to fall into the trap of ruminating and Richard sees everything as black or white. These patterns of thinking obviously were extremely unhelpful. We had to make a conscious effort to focus on the facts we had to hand, where we knew we had control, and direct our action accordingly. Fortunately, both Richard and I are solution driven. After lengthy deliberation, we ultimately decided that there were more options for Anna in the UK. We did as much research as we could, discussed options with our wider family unit, before travelling back to the UK to follow through with the medical assistance we were seeking. By helping us all understand her situation, we could then find appropriate schooling, with the right pastoral support for her. Whilst Anna was keen to go to boarding school; we had mixed feelings. We did not make the decision lightly but hoped we were doing the right thing when we decided that boarding school was the best option at the time.

Anna was diagnosed with Attention Deficit Disorder and Depression. I don't know if you have experience of this but it was a whole new world of which we had no knowledge or understanding and it put an enormous strain on us all. However, following medical advice, we quickly got to grips with setting up processes to help Anna. My family in the UK rallied round and offered maximum support. There was no way we could have managed everything without them and saying we are grateful sounds utterly valueless, considering all they did to look after her best interests and ours.

Times like these also highlight the value of true friends. We all need our tribe who have our back and lift us up when times are tough. Our best friends have stuck by us through thick and thin and have become an extension of our family. How lucky we are to have all these good people in our lives.

A new home

It was at this time, too, that our Landlord in Dubai advised us that he wanted to move back into his villa, so we needed to find another. Whilst we could have asked for more time, Richard and I felt, for many reasons, that it was definitely time to move on but it was a bit of a mad dash to find something we liked. Thankfully, before too long, we found a large, old villa, through a good friend, in a location that suited us well. It needed a great deal of updating but it had potential and ticked a lot of 'boxes' for us. Despite the blistering heat of the summer, the "new" villa was a hive of activity with different tradesmen working in different rooms of the house, in the garden and on the flat roof, racing to get all the repair work completed before our moving date, a few short weeks later. As organised as I was, I hadn't expected Richard to be away, overseas on business, on the day we moved. To be fair, neither had he. So, with George and Anna at School, our lovely Housekeeper and I oversaw the Packers' box up eight years of our lives and transfer all our belongings, including a large number of garden pots and plants, section by section, into the "new" villa where repair work was still being carried out. It wasn't easy keeping four excited Labrador dogs out of the way of the terrified men as they went about their work, nor was it straightforward to complete all the paperwork required when transferring home, without Richard, who was the main point of contact and whose Emirates ID (which had travelled with him) counted for everything! Tougher, too, because I was on crutches, unable to put weight on my left ankle. I don't need to tell you how exhausting it is packing up one home and unpacking it all in the next, as I'm quite sure you have your own experience of this! But, as you know, the relief and joy when it's done, makes all that work worthwhile. It was the best decision we made. Although there are many things in our new home that don't work quite as smoothly as we would prefer – the joy of living in an older villa! - we all love it and are happy here.

A new school

Just as we were getting settled in, we had confirmation that a lovely school in UK was ready to support Anna, as soon as we could arrange it. With great help from my sister-in-law, Lucy, we organised everything as quickly and effectively as we could. Anna was excited and we were hopeful that this would give her the special attention and care that she needed at this time. Incredibly, the timing coincided with my ankle replacement surgery. Another round of packing and before we knew it, Richard and I returned to UK with Anna. Since George was studying hard, he was happy to remain in Dubai with our wonderful Housekeeper and our best friends keeping a watchful eye.

First and foremost, on our agenda, was settling Anna into her new school. We were tense; Anna was a little guarded but she was certain that she wanted to be there. Richard and I hoped we were doing the right thing by our daughter. We were glad to be in the UK just in case.

A new ankle

Three days later, I had to go into hospital for my thirteenth surgery - one of the most significant of them all. Since my mind had been filled with Anna, I had had no time to give much thought to the surgery and having had little sleep in the run up to the operation, the thought of being knocked out for several hours, sounded far more of a reward than an apprehension!

Mr Goldberg and his team did a remarkable job. Despite having to go through nine toolboxes to find the right screwdriver to remove the existing screws in my left ankle, a new plastic and titanium ankle joint, was screwed into the joints of my foot and lower leg, replacing my defunct ankle. The miracle of cutting-edge procedures and a fantastic surgeon gave me new possibilities.

Shortly after I came out of hospital, Richard returned to Dubai to work and to be with George. I was lucky to have my Parents looking after me and my brother nearby. Being in the UK for the first few weeks, enabled me to be nearer Anna. I have to say, as a mother, the pain in my leg was overshadowed by my concern for her. It was a difficult time for Anna, and Richard and I felt anxious on her behalf.

With all the surgical procedures my ankle had had to date, you will be unsurprised, I think, that it was taking its time to heal. In a heavy cast, requiring regular check-ups at the hospital in London, I became adept at hopping through the icy winter weather on my crutches, finding innovative ways to keep my exposed toes covered and dry, though not very warm! I hadn't realised how the cold would affect the metal in my legs and my right ankle (with that internal Meccano structure) felt unbelievably uncomfortable - as though my leg was filled with icy water. Have you ever experienced anything like that? Such a peculiar feeling! Gradually my newest wound began to mend and a few weeks before School Christmas holidays, I was given the all-clear to travel home. Equipped with my crutches, a new open cast, lots of medication and a list of rules about what I could and couldn't do, I was able to fly home.

It was good to be back with the boys and our excitable dogs, fussed over by our Housekeeper and connecting with my close friends. The Dubai sunshine was uplifting, my chilblains started recovering in the warm weather and I felt optimistic organising Christmas, knowing that Anna would be following shortly. It's amazing how we can find little pockets of happiness, even in difficult times.

The hits just keep on coming

My new ankle joint was settling very well but the surrounding soft tissue was still a tangled mess following the accident and was refusing to cooperate with the new movement. My foot felt as though a metal vice was tightly gripping each side of my ankle when I tried to walk. A harsh pinching pain. I was also experiencing nasty tingling in my foot – a sort of pins and needles, where the nerves, caught in the unyielding tissue, were being restricted. Follow up surgery was on the cards, this time to release and lengthen my Achilles tendon and free the trapped nerves. Like a petulant child, my right ankle also began to pain more than usual. I think it was fed up with taking the extra strain. It was time for another trip to Theatre.

George, hoping to fulfil a lifelong ambition of becoming a pilot, had been invited to visit FTE (Flight Training Europe), a well-respected Flight School based in Southern Spain, with a view to applying for a position on the Cadet Training programme. Richard and I decided to accompany him so that we could also get a feeling of the Flight School, with the intention that I would travel on to the UK, afterwards, to have my surgery.

Four weeks prior to travelling, a routine gynaecological appointment, rather threw a spanner in the works when it revealed an issue that would require an urgent hysterectomy! Can you believe it?! I have to say it came as a big surprise to me. My wonderful gynaecologist was quite amazed that I wasn't in pain but truly, I had so much on my mind that I really hadn't noticed. Since the surgery needed to be performed swiftly, I had little choice but to get it over with as quickly as possible, knowing that I had a trip to Spain imminently, as well as the next operation on my ankle - and I needed to heal fast!

I was whizzed into hospital that weekend, my gynaecologist rescheduled everything to do the operation. The surgery turned out to be a little complicated but all was well. I was released within 48 hours. If you've had surgery on your abdomen you will probably recall that it feels initially as though your abdomen has somehow been attached to your knees, and for the first few days, I found it uncomfortable trying to stand upright. Thankfully, with keyhole surgery, the downtime is much less. I rested at home and caught up with all my work administration and training reports, so that I was up to date with everything before I left for UK.

Thankfully, I was given confirmation that I was fit enough to travel to Spain, two weeks later. Obviously, I had to take things carefully. I'm very grateful that I have a strong constitution – a lifetime of regular exercise has kept me fit and strong!

The trip was highly successful, George knew that the Flight School would be the right choice for him and we could understand why. He was excited and we were excited for him. Being summertime, the weather was stunningly beautiful and we enjoyed every minute of our short time spent in Jerez and the surrounding areas of Cadiz and Seville. It was blissful to have something happy and positive to fill our minds with.

Within a few days, I separated from the boys in Madrid airport and flew on to the UK to stay with my Parents. Lovely as it was to see them, I was back in hospital before I knew it. This time Mr Goldberg was working in Theatre together with Mr Marco Senisi - an excellent nerve surgeon. I knew I'd be in good hands and had very little apprehension about the surgery. Post-surgery was a slightly different matter. I was in a lot of discomfort. Mr Goldberg had lengthened my Achilles by 30mm and Mr Sinisi had 'reset' the nerves which had become knotted together with the tendons and ligaments, since my accident. The longer-term forecast was positive; in the short term, I had to cope with terrible muscle cramps. If you've ever experienced that sudden, excruciating grip of pain when cramp takes hold and renders you immobile for a while, you will understand the agonising sensation I was feeling. My main problem was that following the surgery, the cramp only ever dulled into a spasmodic twitching before contracting all over again. Being in a cast, I was unable to stretch out those tightly clenched muscles; it was debilitating. I'm not one to resort to tears easily but for the first time, in a very long time, I actually cried with the pain. I was grateful that the nerves in my foot were, at that point, completely numb, so thankfully they didn't really add to the soreness. The sharp ache from my ankle to the back of my knee, was miserable and exhausting. Mr Goldberg and Mr Sinisi kept a close eye on me and helped me get the pain under control. To distract myself from the pain I tried to think of other things but my mind struggled to stay positive. I was feeling very sorry for myself. I found it hard to relax, let alone sleep. The lovely few days we had spent in Spain, seemed months ago! I know I'm not good at relaxing at the best of times but I have also become aware of the negative effect of stress on my body and that it delays my wounds from healing.

"I didn't come this far, to only come this far"

I forced myself to stop wallowing in self-pity. Of course, being in pain tends to narrow your positive view of the world but getting on top of that helped considerably. I think that part of my problem was that I was in hospital, far away from family and friends. I can slip back into in good spirits very quickly when I have my people around me. I had to work harder to get out of victim zone in the quiet of my room, without my tribe making me laugh and chatting about their day. But what you dwell on is what you become, so I practised every mindset technique I knew, to try and get back on top again. It was tough but nothing changes without effort. I found that some strategies worked better than others. What helped me the most? Focus on keeping perspective. No catastrophising! No ruminating! Challenging and reframing the stories I was telling myself. Hunting for silver linings. Keeping a Victory list - even though the "wins" were very small. I'm not going to pretend this is easy to do, especially when you feel really low, but I can *promise* you it IS possible and before long, I felt a whole lot better. My natural optimism slipped back into place, it became easier to put the silver back into silver linings and by refocusing on my *Circle of Influence*, I felt more positive and more in control. And there is no doubt, once I was back amongst family and friends, life felt much more buoyant.

Chapter 5
LIFE'S GIFTS – FAMILY AND FRIENDS

Finding your tribe, a feeling of belonging

"I get by with a little help from my friends". The Beatles

A tribe: people who share commonalities or possess the traits we aspire to and provide support.

I am energised by being around people and I can say with assurance that the social and emotional support I have from my family, friends and colleagues has played a vital role in my ability to thrive in the many stressful situations I have found myself in.

As humans we are social creatures. To thrive in life, we need meaningful connections with others, to feel we belong and have a purpose, both in our personal life and at work. As Don Clifton says: *"relationships help us define who we are and what we can become. Most of us can trace our successes to pivotal relationships"*.

Having been an expat for most of my life – growing up in Africa, going to boarding school, living in different countries as an adult, as well as working with different groups and organisations across the globe, it has always been important to me to feel accepted as part of a community, to have consistent, good people around me whom I can relate to, have fun with, share common interests, offer my support to, and feel supported in return. This sense of belonging has boosted the quality of my life. I strongly believe, that being part of a tribe is fundamental to our individual and collective happiness.

Our earliest ancestors clustered together in groups to survive – a shared connection and collective identity, defining *us* versus *them*. Nowadays, we get to choose the people, our tribe, that we want to identify with. In fact, we may belong to several tribes, each contributing to the development of our personal and professional growth and wellbeing. I like to think of my *personal tribe* as closer friends whom I have formed a close bond with, and whilst my authentic style is still the same whomever I am with, the nature of our relationship is fundamentally different to that with my professional colleagues.

Have you given much thought to your tribe?

Who are you surrounding yourself with?

Tribes are made up of all the individuals you want to spend your time with, because they each bring unique value to your life, reflect your values and morals, energise and inspire you, support you and bring you happiness. They may know each other, or they may not. Your tribes will shift and evolve as you grow through life, as your circumstances change and your paths move in different directions.

I enjoy people, no matter who they are or where they are from, as long as they are their authentic self. I'm not really impressed by fancy acts, airs and graces. Those whom I have chosen to be in my tribes each add something positive to my life and vary widely in culture, age and professional success. I have had the pleasure of many good friendships since I was a young child and some of these dear people are among my valued inner circle all these years later. I cherish a close handful of friends and family who love, challenge, accept and support me, flaws and all. And through my business and social networks, I have great people whom I can count on to spur my professional growth.

What do you look for in your tribes? What's important to you? I like to be with people who push me to be my best self. I look for individuals with complementary strengths to mine, divergent thinkers who encourage me to see different perspectives and alternative routes to achieve an objective. With my number one CliftonStrengths® theme, Maximiser®, I'm committed to pursuing excellence, so I love to think that this enables me to choose the *best* possible options! When you think about your friendships, where does each person add value for you? What makes your tribe successful? Where might you need more support?

Good quality friendships play a significant role in our wellbeing - from increasing our sense of belonging and promoting our self-esteem, to boosting our happiness. Studies have proven that close, supportive relationships within and outside our family, are a primary factor in resilience. Friendship has been found to extend a person's life expectancy - even lowering various health risks, like heart disease, and serves to protect us in times of stress or depression. Science indicates that the stronger your friendships are, the greater your resilience will be in difficult times.

'No man is an island'

No one wants to feel isolated and alone. Whilst technology ensures that the world is more interconnected than ever before, research reveals that loneliness is on the increase. As the current climate compels us to work remotely, feelings of isolation and lack of meaningful social connection has led to anxiety and depression. Whilst employers are introducing incentives to address this, now more than ever, it is necessary for all of us to reach out, beyond our tribe, to encourage emotional security and wellbeing in others within our networks.

If you are feeling lonely, or disconnected from your colleagues, do find opportunities to reach out to likeminded people who share your passions – it could be work related, or through your hobbies. None of us like feeling vulnerable but reaching out doesn't mean you have to pour your heart out and spill your deepest lows. There is no shame in acknowledging that you feel isolated and need greater social connection. Compile a list of people whom you trust, those who you know you can talk to in times of need, so that when you feel lonely you can reach out to someone on it. Whilst social media definitely has its drawbacks, it can be a useful tool to connect with others. Use it to your advantage for finding business networks or social groups. Focus on the small things in your *Circle of Influence,* that can help you feel more positive and included. Isolation is toxic for our health. The simple truth is that we don't do as well on our own, as we can do together.

Your inner circle

Who has your back when the chips are down?

Who really gets you?

It is true that *"hard times will always reveal true friends".* I found out pretty quickly who was superficial and who was a keeper following my accident. You may have a wide network of acquaintances and friends but when you recall a difficult time in your life, I'm sure you can bring to mind which of them were there to lift you up and offer support.

We all need people in our life that understand what we are going through, whom we can be vulnerable around and share our deepest emotions, without fear of judgment.

There is no doubt that I have overcome so much trauma because I have been lucky to have excellent people around me. Whilst some of my closest friends are scattered across the globe, they have a big impact on how I feel and how I cope. Repeatedly, they have seen me at my lowest, supported me through each stage and helped me manage the most basic things. They've sat by my bedside, held my hand, cheered me on and made me laugh. Together, they've helped me celebrate my wins. I feel blessed. My life is richer for them.

It's important to evaluate the people you spend time with. When it comes to building relationships, you often get what you give. Have you considered what value you bring? What support you offer? I've learned over the years how important it is to nurture good relationships. Friendship is a two-way street. How are you nurturing yours?

Know your frenemies!

"You may be the juiciest, ripest peach in the world but there will still be someone who hates peaches". Dita von Tees

It may, or may not, surprise you to know that not everyone is rooting for you to win! Frenemies are so called "friends" who don't support or help you. They may be pleasant to your face and even appear warm and friendly, but they can make you feel small, whilst boosting their own sense of importance and diminishing you and your achievements to others. Male or female, frenemies are surprisingly common. It's human nature to judge and compare oneself to others but some people will see your success as a threat to themselves, feel envious and resentful, and choose to stab you in the back when they can.

Can you identify someone who fits this description? I know I can! I think most of us have encountered a frenemy or two, over the years. It's critical to be aware of who these people are and weed them out of your life as far as possible. Unfortunately, in this respect, research finds that 84% of women admit to being surrounded by frenemies because they don't want anyone to think they aren't nice people! There is no doubt, I have found it easier to be discerning with age. We put enough pressure on ourselves to be the best we can be, don't allow any so called 'friend' to cause you feel less than you are. Fickle friends are toxic.

Be selective. The tribe we affiliate ourselves with largely determines our success and happiness. Choose your tribe carefully and surround yourself with people who help you succeed.

There is power in the pack

Collaboration and connection will always play a role in our success. Think about your wider network. Where might there be an opportunity to collaborate, to combine strengths, to think creatively and maximise your opportunities to thrive in this demanding environment? We are never too old to make new friends and develop new tribes. Where might your powerful partnerships be? As you build your network never forget that you are also part of someone's network too. Think about what value you bring to them. If you have people who believe in you, you can go far together.

Harvard's 80-year study on emotional well-being and adult development found that good relationships are the single most important component for living a long, successful and happy life. It's the people we surround ourselves with, who help us grow to become our best self. You and I have no idea how long we will grace this planet but as Steve Jobs pointed out: *our time is limited;* so let's ensure we spend it with the right people!

Chapter 6
WHEN YOU HIT ROCK BOTTOM, THE ONLY WAY IS UP

Hitting the bottom

When my Father, the centre of my universe, died, my world crumbled. If you have lost someone very dear to you, you will know exactly how terrible it feels.

I had been back in UK over Summer, with my family, having had yet another surgery on my ankle and was staying with my Parents. My ankle was so compromised following so many operations, it didn't want to heal. Unfortunately, with an ankle replacement screwed into the fragile bones in my leg and foot, an infection is the last thing I needed, so when the stitches refused to hold the wound together, it became an urgent concern. Richard was in London, at a meeting, so my darling Dad drove me to London, to the hospital.

I was speedily hooked up to a drip of antibiotics and given a cocktail of other drugs to try and stave off further problems. A special pump was attached to the damaged tissue of my ankle to remove fluid and increase blood flow and healing. My leg was painful; whilst part of my foot was numb, I was getting muscle cramps and pins and needles from the nerve damage, from the back of my knee down to my toes. The cocktail of meds made me feel dizzy and rather sick. For once, I was glad to be in bed. The surgeons and the medical team were highly attentive.

Despite this latest chink in my armour, we were able to find the humour in the situation. The surgeons were brainstorming healing options for my leg. Amongst the various ideas, were Botox and plastic surgery. I have to say, this did make me laugh...when I think of Botox and plastic surgery, ankles never come to mind! I'm sure you'll agree! (Funnily enough, I have needed the help of a Plastic Surgeon and team on several occasions and *every* time, the insurance company, obviously also having the same thought process, has queried which bits of me require plastic surgery and why!).

Thankfully, my leg started responding to treatment and the Plastic Surgeon and Mr. Goldberg decided, after a few days, that I could go home if I kept my leg raised, though I had to return every second day to get the wound checked.

I was relieved to be out of hospital but that was short lived. My Dad announced the next morning that he felt very peculiar but couldn't figure what was wrong. Richard and my mother took him straight to A&E and they felt it best to keep him in and run some tests. Once he was settled, we all went in to see him. He felt unwell but as usual was in good humour. All seemed ok. That was Saturday. We were concerned but had no cause for alarm; tests were being carried out; Dad was in safe hands. Sunday, little change. On Monday morning, Dad had a cardiac arrest. Something called a cardiac tamponade. I hadn't heard of it before. The doctors said he couldn't survive but my goodness did he fight to stay alive. Our whole family, shocked, moved into the hospital and took turns by his side. We didn't sleep; we couldn't. If you've been in this distressing situation, I don't need to tell you about that sick feeling you get because you're in unknown territory, you have no control and even though you are aware of what the likely outcome is, you desperately and unrealistically want that person you love, to magically pull through.

At dawn, the following morning, Richard drove me to London. (Mr Goldberg offered to see me very early under the circumstances). Unfortunately, the wound was not settling – stress plays havoc where it can - but they understood that I was keen to get back to my Father, so Mr Goldberg and his team carefully repacked my ankle for the next couple of days. I was in a lot of discomfort but my mind was full of Dad and so I was able to mentally block most of the pain in my leg.

My Dad's medical team couldn't believe his tenacity to survive. His situation was, unfortunately, impossible to overcome but they did everything they could to help him. I will always be so grateful to them. We were all with Dad when he died. Dad always loved a party so we were determined that he would leave this world in the happiest way we could make possible. With the extended family gathered around him (we are a big family!), all of us recalling joyful times and sharing a Heineken or two (I'll explain the relevance of this!), we filled his final hours with as much good cheer as we could. But the utter heartbreak was indescribable. I feel that crushing grief all over again as I write this.

But, as desolate as we were because he had gone, the situation wasn't going to change and we had to get through it. As the elder child, rightly or wrongly, I felt it my responsibility to shoulder everything for my Mum. Of course, the family came together and between us, we managed to take care of everything. Living at my parent's house I was able to hobble about on my crutches and ensure my Mum didn't have to worry about anything other than dealing with her grief. We are a stoic family and were all determined to be as positively proactive as we could be.

My Dad

I'd like to take a couple of minutes to share my Father with you because he was fundamental in my life.

Dad was a big man, over 6 feet in height, with a charismatic personality. Possessing a great sense of humour and a knack for storytelling, he drew people to him. His job with Unilever and the Breweries took us, as a family, to West Africa; the beginning of a long, distinguished career for Dad, spanning 30 years. Africa was my Father's passion and, as Chairman of the Breweries, so was beer! He travelled extensively, adored his work and built a huge network of business connections and friends, even meeting with the President of Sierra Leone, Pa Siaka Stevens, on a regular basis. I think my Father knew more about Africa than most Africans! It's said that once you spend time in Africa, it becomes part of your soul. Africa was imprinted on my Dad's soul, just as it is on mine, and my Brother's.

Despite the seniority of his position, Dad always remained down to earth, humble and respected by everyone. He looked after his people. He always offered fair advice when we asked and was an astute mentor to me throughout my career. I learned what good leadership looked like, long before I trained as a leader myself. The most important values Dad instilled in us were to be kind and fair, to have a sense of fun and never to take ourselves too seriously - something I try to remember every day and it always comes to front of mind whenever I feel a little overwhelmed. It helps me re-gain perspective.

We received countless messages and calls from around the world following my Dad's demise and more than 100 people came to celebrate his life, with us. It was heart-warming and brought a streak of sunny happiness at such a bleak time.

The lowest point

I'm sure you will think it unsurprising that one early morning, a couple of weeks after my Dad's funeral, I had a complete meltdown.

My ankle wound had reopened, I was taking very strong medication but still in a lot of discomfort. I hadn't been able to sleep for weeks and the utter misery of losing my Father was completely crushing. I cried and cried and thought my world would never be right again. I felt angry that I had so much to deal with; pressure of trying to shoulder so much responsibility, even though I knew I didn't have to do it on my own. I was sick and tired of the constant pain in my legs, the repetitive tendonitis in my shoulders from being stuck endlessly on crutches, my fingers were getting stiff and sore in the damp English weather and my wrists constantly ached. I could visualise myself sinking to the bottom of a swimming pool and just sitting there, closed off from the world. Richard, not used to seeing me like this, was not sure how to react but accepted I needed this time for myself. I allowed myself some "sorry for me" time. Everyone needs that.

Understanding your emotion and learning to let go

But the truth is that things don't just disappear on their own. If you don't change your thought patterns, or the situation, it will continue to trigger you. Emotional avoidance is harmful. Unless you can allow yourself to acknowledge that emotional pain, you can't begin to heal. What you *do* with that hurt, is more important than the hurt itself. The first step in dealing with it is to recognise it, give it a name. Then get it out of your system – shout, cry, talk to someone, write a journal; whatever works best for you... but get it out. That's what I did and what I do each time I feel in a low place because until we can release the fear, the anger, the loss, the blame...that pain will end up becoming your identity and you will sabotage your ability to move on.

Living a life of happiness and positivity, rather than being a victim of circumstance, is our choice. The only way you can accept new joy and happiness into your life is to make space for it. If your heart is full-up with angst, how can you be open to anything new? You need to make the commitment to "let it go." I will share more about this in a little while.

Getting back up

I can't say that leaving my Mum, Anna and the rest of my family was easy after such a sorrowful time. Neither was travelling back with another heavy cast on my ankle. What made it particularly difficult was that the company I was working with had an urgent request. There was a large teambuilding event - a singing event – in Ras Al Khaimah (one of the other Emirates in the UAE), the morning after I returned. Being the only person who facilitated this event (I sing!), it was with great reluctance that they asked me if I could do it. It was a Friday event (weekend here in Dubai); 7am start - I would return to Dubai only a few hours beforehand – and it happened to be my Birthday. I love my work and am highly motivated but did I want to do this? No. One of my top CliftonStrengths® is Responsibility®. It kicked in and compelled me to say "yes" regardless of my situation. But I still cried. I was tired, in pain, on crutches, grieving for my Dad and still agreed to do it! You probably think, like my family, that it was a foolish idea. You are probably right. But once I'd made that decision, I just focused on what needed to be done. (Luckily Focus® is another of my key strengths).

Just as the sun was rising, a dear colleague arrived in her car, armed with champagne and flowers from the Company and drove me up to the venue. It's not easy motivating a large team of employees who had to get up early on a weekend morning, to do a team building activity when they'd rather be in bed, following a late night the evening before. You need to pull out the stops in order to energise them to jump about, dance and sing together in full voice. Now imagine dominating the stage and building their excitement, whilst on crutches, with your leg in a heavy cast. What an image! But I found my big energy and despite my reservation, my colleague and I pulled it off with gusto and delighted them all.

And actually, I felt damned proud of myself for forcing myself out of self-pity zone. I need to feel a sense of purpose and meaning in my life – I believe we all do - and this turned out to be the right medicine to get me back on track.

As I keep saying when life knocks you down, you don't bounce back; you dig deep and practice the strategies and you lean on your inner strengths to get back up each time. And it happens.

Our feelings are legitimate but they are a gauge. They can guide our actions but we need to take responsibility for the choices we make and our subsequent behaviour, or else our feelings can derail us. Being a victim can feel self-indulgently good for a bit but actually you will come to see that the world moves on... your friends, family, colleagues; the only person stuck is you. I've learned how important it is to focus on directing your attention on what you can do and where you can create positive impact.

Family focus

If you live a distance from your loved ones, you will know how guilty and sad you feel when they need you and you are far away. After Dad died, I phoned my Mum every night for several months to check in on her, just to be sure she was ok. Having had a life partner for more than 50 years, I could only imagine how strange it must be for her. My parents had a very traditional marriage, so my Dad managed all the finances and my Mum managed the home and everything related to it, including us. (Incidentally, I'm known as the "Minister of the Interior"! I wonder where I inherited that trait from?!). Mum was at a loss as to what needed to be done on the financial front, as Dad's demise was so unexpected, and it took time for us all to help her find her feet. But she is amazing. Sad and lonely as she was, she was determined to get to grips with as much as she could and I admire her resilience.

Mum and Anna were due to fly to Dubai to stay with us for Christmas. In the few weeks before they arrived, Richard and I were finalising our end of year accountabilities - business commitments, clients and get organised at home. At the time, I was working in Abu Dhabi and, in all places, a hospital! I was there to run a training journey for a lovely group of young managers. The funny part was that the training room was just a couple of doors down from the Orthopaedic department. *Every day for a week* as I passed it, in my Air boot and on crutches, a different person stopped me, insistent that I was going in the wrong direction, convinced that I was a patient! It did make us all laugh!

Now, I don't know about you, but however prepared I am, Christmas always arrives faster than I anticipate! This year was no exception and it seemed there was a big rush to get stuff done before Anna and Mum joined us, both arriving a couple of days apart. Mum's first flight on her own, incredible when I think of how much time my Parents spent travelling around the world, in their lives. We had arranged a 'Meet and Greet' service but Mum was so busy "getting on with it" she didn't even notice her name and escort and came through customs to meet us on her own! It was lovely to see her but it did seem strange, seeing her arrive without Dad.

It was good to have Anna home. She was still trying to settle into School life and we were keeping an anxious eye on how she was coping. George was studying hard for exams. We were looking forward to the break.

I'm sure like me, you look forward to enjoying time with family and friends at the end of the year. Do you have children? Are there traditional things you like to do together? When our children were little, they would bake cookies, decorate them and string them up on ribbons, as decorations on Christmas Eve. It was always one huge mess in the kitchen, icing and sprinkles everywhere and our four rather greedy Labradors desperately hoping that the children would drop the lot! Now George and Anna are rather grown up but we still like to enjoy the magic of Christmas, hanging stockings and baking treats for Santa and the reindeers! And every Christmas Eve since they were both tiny, I have read the poem *"'Twas the Night Before Christmas"*. They used to find it terribly exciting when they were small and used to recite it with me; now I read it out loud whilst everyone's enjoying a glass of Christmas Cheer before bed! Such are the changes when your little ones become adult!

This year, specifically, we all made a very big effort to focus on the good things, reflect on our sadness with grace and hunt for the silver linings in our melancholy moments. It wasn't easy because my Dad had been such a life force that we missed him terribly. The thought that gave us most comfort was that Dad had loved life and had lived his to the fullest, with purpose and passion. A life of direction and meaning. I believe this is fundamental to our well-being and achievement in life.

Surrounding ourselves with dear friends, sunshine and good food helped enormously. Mum relaxed and rested. It was such a healing time.

The end of every year always brings reflection, gratitude and hope. This year had been a rough year in so many ways but I was grateful that we had weathered it and got through.

In agreement with Marcus Buckingham, "*You can find energising moments in each aspect of your life, but to do so you must learn how to catch them...and to allow yourself to follow where they lead*".

A point for reflection: *Struggles and loss are unavoidable but life becomes more meaningful when you know what you live and stand for.*

A question for consideration: *What fuels your motivation in life?*

Resilient responses: *To help you clarify your life purpose and find fulfilment in your life, please see* **Tools for Flourishing: Knowing Your Purpose.**

Chapter 7
OWN YOUR PERSONAL POWER

A positive approach

Throughout my ordeal, people have often asked how I remain so resilient, full of energy and buoyant, despite facing hurdle after hurdle.

Quite honestly, I hadn't given this much thought, assuming the way I was coping with the obstacles in my life, was similar to the reaction of others in similar situations. On reflection, I recognised that I was somehow managing each setback with some deep-seated positivity which I didn't really understand, nor could I quite figure out what I was actually *doing* differently to anyone else. It was curiosity that saw me signing up to learn about positive psychology from the great Barbara Fredrickson, *Psychologist and Professor of Positive Emotion,* and what an impact it had on me! Clarity at last! I was able to recognise the strategies I was using instinctively; understand why I was doing what I did. I was hooked! For the next few years, I read, I studied more (and I still continue to learn and study!) and I used myself as the 'guinea pig' on which to practise different techniques as I went along.

Let me share some of these insights with you.

We hear and read about "being positive" so often that it can sound a bit of a cliché but it really does have its benefits. Positive emotions undo the lingering effects of negative emotions and make you feel calmer and happier.

When it comes down to how we experience life, we have two clear options before us - we can either experience life in a downward spiral where negativity rules our thoughts and we feel unhappy, or in an upward spiral where positivity reigns and we feel good.

You have the choice on how you prefer to live and what I've learned since my accident, is that whether you make yourself happy or depressed, the amount of effort is the same.

Adversity typically induces strong negative responses that can hijack your rational thinking and shrink your resilience, so in order to live a happier life, the first thing is learning to understand and manage your negative feelings, so you can react to your situation in way that is helpful to you.

The positive impact of negative emotions

Let's be clear here, negative emotions exist to keep us safe. We are innately wired to stay away from threat and our negative emotions serve to warn us of possible dangers and induce us into action – run for cover (flight), fight back, or freeze – to stay out of harm's way. So far so good but what's important here for our overall wellbeing, is how we approach our reactions in these situations.

Masking emotions can be harmful to our overall health, draining our energy, leading to burnout and emotional imbalance. Whilst we certainly don't want to stay in a negative state for longer than necessary, it's important to acknowledge the emotions we are feeling and decode what they are telling us. Negative emotions can put us in touch with our deeper selves- a deeper self-awareness and wisdom, from which we can learn how to respond rationally rather than react emotionally.

There are times when it is necessary for us to experience negative feelings in order to move forwards with a positive focus. Managed healthily, they can be motivators for positive action; harnessed and aimed productively to move you towards what benefits you.

There are so many emotions which can cause you to feel miserable and sad, that can undermine your self-confidence and diminish you. I'm sure you can call to mind plenty that you have experienced yourself. I am just going to draw your attention to a few examples to illustrate how they can contribute to our *wellbeing*.

Let's start with *Grief.* I'm sure there have been times in your life when, like me, you have faced loss. The pain can be completely overwhelming; your emotional balance is thrown into turmoil. It drags you through an expanse of emotions that come and go unexpectedly and catch you out when you're least expecting it. I feel that coping with loss is one of life's biggest challenges. Loss can appear in many ways -the death of a loved one, an end of a relationship, loss of income, medical decline...We don't get over loss or trauma, we have to learn to adjust to living with it. It's a very individual experience but to heal, we have to feel. We need to grieve, so we can process, learn to accept and that in turn helps us to move forwards and whilst we may never forget, I've learned that it *is* possible to find joy in our lives once again.

With all the demands we place on ourselves, it's hard not to get overwhelmed every now and again. I'm sure, like me, you have been – or perhaps are going through - stages in your life where worry, stress and apprehension dominate. *Anxiety* can be an indication that some areas of our life are off track and need adjusting. Bringing an awareness to our current situation, anxiety alerts us to the fact that we may need to make some necessary changes. It can spur us into problem solving, finding alternative, positive solutions for our concerns.

Whilst being overly aggressive is clearly destructive, *Anger* can bring some advantages. Channelled effectively, it can activate us towards serving specific goals. It can motivate higher performance, increase our persistence to accomplish a task, spark our creativity and promote justice.

Fear, heavily linked with our self-preservation, serves to point out why our world can be a scary place. It can help us stay in the present moment and focus on what needs to be done, snapping us into being fully alert. Facing our fears can help us navigate potential dangers, successfully. I believe fear and courage go hand in hand. Nothing great can be accomplished without facing fear. Getting out of our comfort zone, pushing past our uncertainty and having the courage to move forwards into the unknown. To be successful in any endeavour, we have to do something worthy of fear.

Then there's *Guilt*. As Dr David Burns says: "*Guilt serves as a powerful social function in terms of policing our behaviour*". Guilt makes us more socially aware. It can give us the motivation to make amends and repair wrongdoing.

Whatever the negative emotion that we are experiencing, feeling bad really sucks! It's easy to play the victim and the blame game but none of us want to get stuck in unhealthy negative emotions which are self-defeating and sabotage our move towards a happy, purposeful life. If you can infuse those negative situations with positive meaning, each time they arise, these emotions can serve to enhance your ability to cope with whatever life throws at you.

This is something I have taught myself to do. When I feel low, I ask myself: *what exactly is challenging me? What am I being fearful of?* It gets me to the core of the situation and then I figure out how I can move those concerns into my *Circle of Influence;* what positive action I can take to move forwards. It puts me into the driving seat and this feeling of empowerment helps me to recover more quickly after each setback.

An important lesson I've learned: whatever your challenge and however bad you feel, you need to be firmly in the driving seat to be sure that you have the power to influence your life so that you flourish.

Promoting positivity

Whilst studying under Professor Fredrickson, I learned that the difference between people who are flourishing and those who aren't, lies in the magnitude of positive emotions they are able to self-generate every day.

Why?

When we feel threatened, our repertoire of responses tends to narrow so we can respond quickly to our situation. What I learned from her *Broaden and Build Theory*, is that positive emotions widen our ability to think more creatively and see greater options for problem solving. In other words, when we feel more positive emotions to negative ones, we are going to handle difficult situations more easily.

The more we deliberately practice selecting a positive thought to dwell on, as opposed to a negative, self-defeating one, it becomes easier for us to reach for those positive thoughts, even in adverse situations. Micro-moments of positivity amass over time, building our repertoire of resources. This empowers us to think more optimistically and to develop enduring strengths and skills, which set us on that life enhancing, upward spiral where we flourish.

I'm not going to pretend this is easy - especially if positivity isn't one of your strengths; it does take practice. But I can assure you that it is really worth the effort! I've been honing this skill for several years and it has made a huge impact on how I manage when the going gets tough.

Did you know that your brain cannot hold a negative thought and positive one, simultaneously? Try it and see...

You can think of one and then the other in quick sequence but not the two together!

Since a negative belief narrows your thinking but a positive one uplifts you and helps dampen down negative emotions, don't you think it makes sense, therefore, to practice as many positive thoughts that you can?

Positivity® happens to be one of my top 10 Gallup® CliftonStrengths® and, as you know, I am a natural optimist, but whether or not positivity is one of your strengths, I think it's fair to say that when you feel very challenged it still can take every ounce of determination to summon up positive thoughts and not allow negative thinking patterns to pull you down. I know I've felt that many times.

Here are some strategies that I rely on, to keep me focused on the good things in my life. You may be familiar with them already. How well do you practice them? I'd love to know what works best for you.

Be Mindful: Being aware of my thoughts, emotions, and how I'm feeling both physically and mentally. Paying attention on purpose, so that I can be in control of my situation and not letting my situation control me.

Count my blessings: appreciating the good things. Even when I have tough days, I've learned to graciously recognise that there is always a silver lining and something, or someone, to be thankful for.

***The Three Good Things* exercise**: *Marty Seligman (Father of Positive Psychology)*. Thinking of three positive things that happened in my day. It's an instant happiness boost. I'm no *Pollyanna* but as I mentioned, I can see how practising positive thinking has successfully impacted my ability to cope and feel motivated to get back on track.

Don't dwell on failure: I don't allow myself to become a victim of circumstance. I expect things to get better. If you only expect negative outcomes, you will not see solutions. I know that sometimes it may feel like the universe is out to get you but believe the phrase "this too shall pass". I promise it will get easier and you *will* be able to move on.

Get around positive people: Negativity drains me. I like to be with people who enjoy life, who help me put things into perspective when I feel doubtful and support me when I reach out. Have you got a good support network? Finding your tribe is so important *(As explained in Chapter 5)*.

Boost wellbeing: Finding the time to do the things I love. It balances and counteracts all the demands I place on myself every day (My strength of Achiever® can squeeze 36 hours out of every 24!). When you are feeling tense and upset, it can be all too easy to neglect your own wellbeing. I can be my own worst enemy in this regard. Losing your appetite or overeating, not exercising, not getting enough sleep, drinking too much alcohol, smoking too much and generally driving yourself too hard, are all common reactions to stressful situations. Sound familiar? I drive myself endlessly and have to force myself to take time out and relax. What can you change to boost your wellbeing?

What do you love to do? Sport is always an answer for me; alleviates stress immediately. As does being in the kitchen. I'm well known for baking! I find the whole process therapeutic. When I'm stressed, I cook up a storm and have enough for everyone's freezer. Cakes, pastries and ice cream are top of my list! I make to order!! (I'm sure I'd be the size of a house if I didn't do so much sport!) Change your pace, your scenery, spend time with people you love to be around. It boosts your overall health and resilience.

Act the emotion I want to feel: This may sound a bit dramatic but we actually *feel* a certain way because of the way we *act*. If you want to change that, by altering the way you act, you can induce the relevant emotions in yourself. Actions do influence feelings! There's a quote which sticks in the forefront of my mind, in this respect, by Elizabeth Taylor, where she says: *"Put on some lipstick and pull yourself together"*. I resonate with this well! Having worked in the cosmetics and fashion business at Harrods, in a management capacity, for many years, I guess I associate wearing lipstick with being in a professional environment; it immediately makes me feel cool, calm and collected and I "pull myself together"!

Did you know, even putting on an artificially induced smile can help us feel happier?

How about you? Have you ever been in a situation where you have found that changing your action, changed your emotion?

You may not believe this but when I was a child, I was shy and would feel very uncomfortable going into a room of people who knew each other but might not know me. I would slink in and stand at the side of the room hoping to see someone I knew and could latch on to. I realised over time, that if I wanted to be part of the interesting discussions – and I was dying to join in! - that I needed to make the effort, so on future occasions, I deliberately walked straight into the middle of a busy room with a smile on my face and introduced myself to someone. Whilst my heart pounded at the beginning, I soon felt included in the group and relaxed and enjoyed myself. Now, years on, it feels natural to do that. Amy Cuddy (Social psychologist, known for *How your body language may shape who you are*) talks about *"faking it until you become it"*. I'm proof it works! I spend much of my time as a speaker and professional development consultant, in front of large groups and I love it! Having said that, I am always conscious of that shy person on the side of the room and I make sure that I don't overlook them.

By the way, if you haven't come across Amy Cuddy, I strongly recommend looking up her work. One of her famous "life-hacks" is power posing, to feel more confident. I've known many people who have tried this with success. Do check out her TED talks!

Keep going! Resilience is how we manage each setback. I've been through enough setbacks to know that perseverance is key. Keep working at it. Even if progress slows to a crawl. No matter what, keep going.

You don't need to make giant leaps. Just tiny steps at a time. Being resilient takes practice but unless you start, things wont change and everyone knows that when you keep practicing something you get better at it. Just focus on little things that you can do to move you in the right direction (*Circle of Influence*). Dig into your strengths, you have a free and powerful toolkit of resources that can help you.

Leaning into your Strengths

Have you ever wondered why you love some things more than others?

Why you make the choices you do?

Why you find some things easier to learn?

Why you have chosen a particular career path?

What makes you tick?

You may be surprised to know that most people haven't given this much thought. We get so involved in doing what we do in our everyday life that we rarely hit *PAUSE* to give ourselves the time to self-reflect on who we are, appreciate what makes us great and identify what we need to be at our best

Looking back through my life, I realise that I have always unconsciously played to my strengths but I hadn't appreciated just how powerful they could be, until I had my accident. Since that time, I have discovered, that they are vital in terms of whether we fail, get by, or truly flourish in life. I've found that most people underestimate what they are capable of and rarely give themselves enough credit for what they do. I have learned how much personal influence and sway we have when we understand how to use this inherent toolbox of resources, we have all been blessed with.

Let's talk talent

We are all born with a natural disposition to be better at some things than others. We have an innate toolkit of talents which are completely unique to each of us. Our talents describe us, how we think, feel and behave. Talents influence our choices, direct our actions and are our greatest source of potential and success in life. But most of us underappreciate and undervalue them! Why? Because we are wired to focus on negativity – we tend to have an elephant's memory for what hasn't gone right but usually struggle to remember our successes! We try to fix what doesn't work, rather than build on what we are naturally good at because we assume that which is challenging and difficult, *must* be more valuable to us. We presume that what we do, everyone can do, and we often don't regard what comes easily to us, as special. But it is! Instead of appreciating our talent, we often downplay it; we dismiss compliments...by saying *"Oh, it was nothing!"*. Whaaat?! It obviously meant something to that person and that makes you special.

Your talents are what separate you from the crowd.

To turn your talents into strengths, you must intentionally develop them by adding skills, knowledge and practice. It takes effort, just like it does to build physical strength. As you know, if you want a super fit physique, you've got to get off the sofa. But that said, strengths are things that energise you. They are things you really look forward to doing - you want to keep doing more of them! When I was a runner, I loved it so much that I enjoyed putting in the miles to get stronger and faster. What things do you love to do? Do you give yourself enough time to feed that passion and build your talent?

Your strengths offer you your biggest opportunity for growth. If you invest in something you are naturally good at, your potential is virtually unlimited. The more you invest in those strengths, the better your performance, the more self-confident you feel and the more inspired you are to keep pushing boundaries for yourself. It's an upward spiral that leads you not only to success but a feeling personal accomplishment.

A "rounded" approach

I dislike the fascination people have with being a good all-rounder. Historically, this was associated with status and the idea still exists that to be recognised as intelligent, we should all aim to be well rounded. In my opinion, it robs us of our individual identity and squashes us all into the same box. But being a great all-rounder was highly encouraged and applauded when I was at school; the benchmark for us to be measured against. I bet that if I ask you to think of someone who fits that description, you can envisage one person from your class who was seemingly brilliant at all academic subjects, fluent in 5 languages, outstanding on the playing field and confidently played Beethoven's Piano Concerto No. 5, at school concerts. Ok, possibly a little exaggerated but you get the point. Academic achievements merited you with School credit. Personal strengths were not valued in the same way as they are now, where competence and potential are considered necessary, effective evaluators of performance and future growth. I remember my early leadership skills being interpreted as being bossy (no comments please!), my desire to make things "even better", taken as being intense and fussy, and as for being a chatterbox, well, that would get me nowhere – except into detention! Whilst I did pretty well at school, I remember feeling the frustration of not being able to spend more time on the things that I loved and hating having to spend time on things that I didn't find inspiring and had to work harder at.

The fundamental problem with being an all-rounder is, if you spread your efforts trying to be *everything,* in which area will you gain mastery? How will you ever realise your true talents and become the person you are meant to be?

A bit about Mastery

Today's world is about specialisation. The open secret about the 21st Century is that it is *depth* matters more than spreading yourself thin. If you want to be a master in your field, you must keep looking for opportunities to fine tune your talent, invest in those strengths in the right way and aim them in the right direction. The more you consciously think about your talents, the more you can notice how they contribute to your success and your potential for even greater success!

Growing up in Africa, I had Indian teachers in my early school life, who were quick to pick up on potential. A well-known chatterbox in class, and out of it, and a natural storyteller, they focused my skills in a more constructive direction, had me debating on television, at the age of nine and involved me in public speaking opportunities. By the time I went to boarding school, I had recognised that public speaking was something I was good at and I very much enjoyed. I still love to capture an audience! Over the years, this is a strength that I have capitalised on and used it to my best advantage.

As Dr Seuss said: *Why fit in when you were born to stand out?*

Where do you stand out? What do you want to be known for?

Get clear on what makes you unique. Think about how you naturally approach problems and solutions and the value you bring to situations. What are you great at? How can you create more of that? Think about how you manage setbacks. What do you do that enables you to get through them? Remember, talent needs to be exercised to become a strength. How are you exercising yours? Be confident in who you are and the special value you bring.

Weaknesses and non-talent

Whilst our greatest potential in life starts from a place of strength, that is not a reason to ignore our weaknesses. We all have things we are not good at but it might surprise you to hear that not all of those are necessarily weaknesses. We need to accept that we all have areas of non-talent. We may be impressively clever at many things but we are simply *not* talented in everything. We can learn those things, increase our performance and become competent but they will never become a strength, since strengths begin with a repository of talent. In other words, you can learn do a specific task or action, like dancing, for example, but if it doesn't come naturally to you, you will never look as graceful and fluid as someone who is naturally talented in that area. You only have to watch a programme like *Strictly Come Dancing*, to identify that!

Gallup® describes a weakness as something that gets in the way of our success, so these are things we must identify and learn to manage. I believe our dominant talents give us clues as to what our resilience weaknesses might be. For example, I love to be busy and active; I have an incredible amount of energy and I dash about getting my list of stuff done, on a daily basis, but when, for example, I had to be wheelchair bound, the slowness, inactivity and general inability to get about, frustrated me beyond belief! I fluctuated between impatience with myself for not fixing fast enough, tears because I felt frustrated, victimised, and being short tempered. This wasn't helpful in terms of feeling better, nor did it endear me to the people around me. What I did to mollify the situation, was to do specific daily exercise routines that kept my body strong and energised me and to find activities and tasks which forced me to concentrate on other things. It wasn't easy and I didn't always feel gracious about it but it really helped.

Extraordinary children

Going back to when you were at school, do you remember when you would take your report home for your parents to read? How did they react? Maybe you always had outstanding results but if your situation was anything like mine, you may have had occasions where not all your grades and feedback was quite as remarkable as you might have liked. What was your parents' instinctive reaction? My parents would obviously be pleased with the good grades but zone in, with concern, on areas where I didn't do as well as expected. A *lower grade?! Questionable effort?! What happened here? Why? What should you have done? What didn't you do? How can you improve this? You must try harder in this subject...*There's that negativity bias I was referring to earlier, zoning in on what's wrong rather than what's right! Does this sound familiar to you? Research proves that success will follow when you focus on the better grades and say to your children *What did you do to achieve that? Fantastic! How can you make more of that happen?*

Opportunities for improvement often accentuate the negatives. When you connect your mind to positive things, your mind sees opportunities and possibilities. When you focus your mind on weaknesses and negativity, your mind frames this as a threat and closes off to solutions. And the sting of being criticised lasts significantly longer than the feeling of wellbeing when praised.

As children, we are still discovering ourselves and if you are a parent, I urge you to help your children recognise their natural talent and nurture that in them. Help them to find ways to develop it further, to look for where they can stand out and be extraordinary people. This fast-paced world is creating future opportunities that are outside anything we can imagine. What better gift can we give our children than to help them grow up with the self-confidence of knowing the unique value they bring, where they are most likely to succeed in life and the direction they want to head towards?

As Peter Drucker (Management Consultant) wisely advises, *"It takes far more energy to improve from incompetence to mediocrity than it takes to improve from first-rate performance to excellence."* We get the greatest return on our investment by focusing on our strengths, not from striving to improve our areas of low talent.

The people who truly *thrive* in life are the ones that are continuously using their strengths, whilst doing work that they really value.

How my Strengths have helped me

There is no doubt that understanding my strengths has been a revelation, fuelling my confidence, giving meaning to my life and enabling me to fulfil my purpose. Now I know where my greatest potential is, I know I am on an upward spiral.

I learned through Gallup® that my top CliftonStrengths® theme is Maximiser®– seeing strengths and talent in others (whilst also appreciating my own gracious gifts!) and feeling compelled to elevate this to its highest form for peak performance, greater resilience and self-confidence, so those people can become their best self, part of a successful team, both at work and at home and find more fulfilment in life. I feel excited every time I discover someone's strengths because my mind starts to envisage amazing opportunities for them and I want them to realise just how special they can be.

Whatever goals you may have, your strengths are your pathway to achieving them. They shape your direction for both your professional development and your wellbeing. When you work to your strengths, you are more productive, feel more energised, assured and happy.

It is easy to feel confident when you are not too hard pressed by life but when you are put to the test, you need all your resources, and I promise you, that when it comes to being resilient, you are equipped with the resources to get through any challenge. When it comes to thriving, you need to clarify your own definition of what balance and wellbeing mean to you. Know your strengths, have confidence in who you are. Every day you have a choice to be extraordinary. Make that choice.

As Gallup® has recognised: *There's a connection between who people are and what they do best; what they do best and how they feel; what they feel and how they perform.*

Do you know where your strengths lie? Are you using them in your life? If you're not, then what is it that stops you from doing so?

I encourage you to take the time to understand your strengths; to be confident in what makes you uniquely powerful. You can't improve that which you don't recognise!

Chapter 8
STRENGTH AND COURAGE

"Life is a series of ups and downs. They are known as squats".

I'm not sure where I read this but it made me chuckle. This being so, I must be fighting fit and well ahead of the game!

The reality: "The trick is to enjoy the Ups and have courage during the Downs"

Celebrating the wins

Celebrating the 'wins' is boosting to our morale - even more so when we face challenging, uncertain times. It can be easy to feel overwhelmed when one hurdle seems to be superseded by another and I have found that, without doubt, each little victory seems so much sweeter when contrasting with a backdrop of difficult situations.

Family and work have always been a great source of purposefulness for me and, since my accident, I have become determined to enjoy every win and celebrate every success.

The first win of the year was that George's hard work was paying off. He was invited to the FTE (Flight School Europe) in Jerez, where he aced his interviews and exams. He followed that with excellent A level results a few months later, which secured his place at the flight school. He had consistently worked to his strengths and we were overjoyed that his little boy dream was now becoming his adult reality. We were so excited for him but nothing could match the utter delight he felt.

Another win was my work. It was buzzing for Richard and for me and I was doing a lot of travelling. I was energised and loving the groups of leaders that I was training and seeing such great outcomes. Moreover, I was studying to further develop my positive psychology knowledge and working with Gallup® on strengths-based development. I realised I had found my true passion and I was thrilled to become a Gallup® Certified Strengths Coach. When you understand how your innate toolkit of strengths work together – like different blends, shades and depth of colour – you truly recognise where your personal power is. Studying what is right with you, rather than focusing on what is wrong, is the most motivating, morale building experience! I have recognised that most people have such little idea of how talented they truly are. Like a sponge, I soaked up everything I could learn and practice. I have never felt so inspired.

My ankles, on the other hand were both troubling me - intense cramps and pain during the night, no matter whether I stood, sat, or did physical exercise in my day. Most nights I paced the floor trying to get some relief. The lack of sleep would have been completely debilitating if it wasn't for the fact that my days were so enjoyable. Following discussion with Mr Goldberg, it appeared likely that I would require yet another trip to Theatre. But, in the meantime, I had another small win! I was lucky to meet an excellent orthopaedic specialist who arranged for a special splint and inserts for my shoes so I could walk with less pain, and he gave me some good suggestions for my daily work out, to minimise impact on my lower legs. In actual fact, when he saw my injuries, he couldn't believe that I was able to walk, let alone do sport, but his recommendations were very helpful. My hips also needed a bit of physio to realign, as my stance and gait were compromised. All these things helped enormously but the nightly cramps were determined to persevere.

Knowing that I would be back in a cast once more, and sooner rather than later, we took the opportunity to travel to Valencia with Mum and Anna beforehand. George, having finished all his exams, was off travelling and would meet us there. Yet another win! We had a wonderful holiday. Do you know Valencia? We loved the culture and history of the ancient city, the modern futuristic buildings, the beautiful fine art alongside the street art. It was stunning. We walked miles every day - yes, even with my dodgy legs and trusted crutch! I figured rightly, or wrongly, that if I was going to be in pain at night regardless, I might as well do all the things I wanted to do during my days!

Whilst the family enjoyed some English sunshine in August, I was back on the operating table. There was no doubt that the injuries to my ankles were giving the best surgeons in the world something to deliberate over. I am so lucky to have such an amazing team, led by Mr Goldberg. He continues to find cutting edge methods to keep me upright and enable me to have a decent quality of life. Every surgery brings me new opportunities.

Finding courage in difficult times

With so many positive things to be grateful for, it hit us exceptionally hard when, towards the end of the year, our darling Anna, had a nervous breakdown. Richard and I were utterly shocked. Unforeseen changes at school, a victim of bullying and trying to manage her Attention Deficit Disorder, became overwhelming for her. We were all gutted. She had been really trying so hard and we had been seeing good outcomes. Worried about Anna, unimpressed with how the situation had been managed at the School, relief and concern that Graham, Lucy and their family were shouldering the troubles on our behalf, we had some big decisions to make.

I had just flown back from working in London, tired and foot sore, in a cast, and had literally gone straight into the training room to deliver a course on Innovation, when Richard and I heard the news. My stomach dropped but we had to make quick, rational decisions and I had a group of delegates waiting in the training room, expecting a good learning experience. My mind was racing with concern, I had to keep blocking the thoughts as far as possible, so that I could facilitate that training programme. My inner dialogue completely at odds to what I was calmly doing and saying to the group of young leaders, I thankfully held it together and received great feedback though I really couldn't take it all in. Richard had sorted flights. I went home, re-closed my yet-to-be-unpacked suitcase and we headed straight back to the airport, on an overnight flight to the UK. It was not a relaxing journey and neither of us slept but catastrophising wouldn't help, so we started putting logical plans in place and by doing so, we felt more in control.

I have learned to bear pain for myself but, as a parent, knowing your child is in pain, is gut wrenching. You want to be able to give them something that will take away their pain but Anna's situation wasn't something that we knew how to fix. We needed medical advice. Anna had been permitted to leave hospital and Lucy, God bless her, was looking after Anna for us. After a few days in the UK, in discussion with different medical advisors, it was agreed that we could bring Anna home to recover and heal. She needed us and we needed to be strong for her. We returned to Dubai anxious but determined to help Anna find her confidence once more. It was stressful. Fear of the unknown, Richard and I were filled with anxiety – were we helping her in the best way? Never mind the pain in my ankle, worry kept us both awake every night but we were as proactive and positive as we could be and, within a few weeks of being quietly at home - sleep, good food, fresh air and a fantastic art teacher, who helped Anna connect to her hopes and fears through her art, Anna started to thrive once again. It was a relief indeed.

A second blow followed when we heard that my best friend, Biddi, was diagnosed with cancer. Hearing that word, itself, is fearful. I think our minds instinctively go to dark places, unfortunately conjuring up all sorts of unhelpful images. We want to imagine the best outcome. We want to show support and love especially when it's someone we really care about. I met Biddi when she joined the Training company I worked for. We hit it off straight away and I've always loved her to bits. Hugely caring and kind, very stubborn and unbelievably loyal, she, Mandi and their families – including a vast number of cats - became a big part of our lives. We took our cues from Biddi. Never one to make a fuss, her preference was to keep this quiet. She decided to go home to South Africa to have treatment. We understood that although it was a rare cancer, it was treatable and we all hoped it could be dealt with as quicky and effectively as possible. We were aware that she wouldn't be with us for the latter part of the year, nor the beginning of the new year, but we so wanted her better and it was most urgent that she got the treatment she needed. In this respect, I am grateful for social media – keeping us all connected despite being across the globe from each other. Biddi went through a tough time. We were so glad that she had good people taking care of her. It took several months of treatment and recuperation before she was able to return to us. Her future was worryingly uncertain but for the time being, she was better. And we were grateful indeed.

Making hay whilst the sun shines

Before we knew it, Christmas was suddenly upon us; this time my whole family was coming out to stay and Richard's eldest brother, Peter, was passing through Dubai and would be with us for Christmas and New Year. Do you remember the disruptions in the UK with the Drones that shut down airports and caused complete havoc? Did it affect you in any way? Well, our family were completely caught in it! A few hours of delay to their flight, stretched into 2 days! But then they ALL arrived together – Mum, Graham, Lucy and their three children, George flying in from Spain, and then Peter ...Ohhh, the excitement of seeing them all! With a house full of adults, teenagers and younger children, Christmas was a happy, fun time. How I wished my Dad could have been with us, too. I like to imagine that he's somehow able to watch over us and knows everything that's going on in our lives.

Richard and I travelled back, with Anna, to the UK, for my Mother's milestone Birthday celebration. It was lovely to regroup as a family. Mum, a natural optimist, has learned to thrive through difficulties and I was so proud of everything she had achieved since Dad died. We toasted her, we toasted Dad and it we all had a marvellous celebration.

After deep discussion with all the parties concerned, we had agreed with Anna, that she could return to school. She was feeling positive and ready to move forwards. With lots of rules in place, she settled back in. Richard and I had decided to stay in the UK for the first month after she returned, to be sure she was ok. Anna slipped back into her routine and all appeared to be going well.

And, would you believe it, I needed more surgery on my left ankle?! Both ankles had been competing for attention but the left one was (and still is) much less stable, so Mr Goldberg and Mr Sinisi needed to carry out some more work on the nerves, do a little recutting and deeply inject cortisone. Anything to help with the pain, longer term, and to have more restful nights, was worth another trip to Theatre, in my opinion.

On a cold March day, following my exit from hospital, I was hopping up and down Oxford Street, in London, on my crutches, in a new cast, desperately looking for warm socks or soft boots, to cover my freezing toes. Unbelievably, bitterly cold as it was, London had Summer stock on display – flip flops a plenty but no thick woolly socks! Honestly!! If you know me, you will be familiar with the fact that I am a Doc Martens fan and wear a wide variety of DM boots and shoes - especially since high heels are sadly not for me anymore. I was bitterly disappointed that, this time around, I was unable to get my foot into the new season boots and was trying to feel grateful that I eventually found a pair of open backed Ugg slippers which at least kept my toes warm and didn't hurt my feet.

Digging deep for inner strength

This time around my ankle, so very compromised by all the surgeries, refused to heal. With 5-inch scars all around my ankle, Mr Goldberg said it was like trying to stitch tissue paper. (I have to mention here, that on better days, Richard and I laugh that if I was to have a tattoo, it should be of a tiny pair of scissors and a dotted line circling my ankle, with an inscription reading *"Cut here"*!)

Eventually, when Mr Goldberg was satisfied that I had a Wounds Specialist in place, and that my ankle had mended sufficiently for me to travel, I was allowed to return home. Fortunately, I had a great team here in Dubai, and finally, after 12 weeks of consistent effort and relentless application of sterilized honey treatment, my ankle healed - at least on the outside. It was a highly successful result but, my goodness, it was a terribly painful process! Have you ever experienced this type of treatment? It *stings*! In addition, the nerve pain was horrendous. I was taking very strong medication but it proved very challenging to get the pain under control. To top it all, I had tendonitis, again, in my shoulders from relying heavily on my crutches. Unable to sleep, I felt exhausted and run down. During the day when I was working, I would try to elevate my leg but it wasn't very practical to do this in a training session as I needed to move about the room and I certainly couldn't do it when on a stage, presenting. I like to think I've become pretty tough minded after so much practice but this was a good example that it takes total bloody mindedness and focused effort to get back up and feel in control, when circumstances hit you hard. No way have I ever *"bounced"* back. I've needed to use every strategy and personal resource that I have, to cope with each setback.

During this time Biddi received the devastating news that her cancer had metastasized. It was a terribly dark, unhappy place for her and for all of us who love her.

Whilst battling to overcome the difficulties of this latest surgery, Richard and I had another massive blow. Horrified to hear that Anna was still struggling with the bullying issue and with insufficient management from the School, she had another breakdown, and this time, she was completely defeated. Our first and overriding emotion was fury with the School for not taking care of the situation as they should have. Anna had picked herself up and had been so happy to return...I couldn't bear to think of our baby going through such despair. It was heart wrenching. We blamed ourselves for not getting the situation right in terms of pastoral support... for being too far away. At that point we felt so very much outside our *Circle of Influence* but struggling to get back into that control seat. I can say, without doubt, that I felt crushed, physically and mentally. The nerve pain in my ankle escalated -worry, I guess – and it took every personal resource I had, to focus on what needed to be done and not give up or give in.

I'm so grateful that Richard and I are solution oriented. We needed to be. We had some major, long term decisions to make, along with Lucy and Graham, who were doing everything their end to help. It wasn't right for them feel the strain on our behalf; we recognised we needed to bring Anna home and to find the right help for her here in Dubai. With very troubled hearts we flew back to the UK again.

Fortunately, we got everything organised very well between us all and we brought Anna home. First and foremost, we all needed to press *"pause"* and rest so we could focus clearly on the best options for Anna. Thankfully, Dubai is now set up with more medical professionals than it ever was. We found excellent pastoral help for Anna. Very, very slowly she began to open up and with lots of support, she began to pick herself up. We organised private tutoring, which worked very well and after a few months of being back at home, we saw vast improvement, on every level. Anna started to bloom once more, and with more confidence than she had in years. The relief for us, was massive. Now, with the right support and a confidence in her own ability at School, she is achieving remarkable things. I am so proud of her.

Two key learnings

Firstly, feeling unable to cope is not something to be ashamed of, or hide away from. We all have challenges that can threaten our mental wellbeing at different times in our life. In fact, research reveals 1 in 5 people will need help at some point. Asking for help is important on so many levels. Are you good at reaching out when you need help? So many people, particularly women, and myself included, dislike being perceived as needy, or perhaps fear rejection, and therefore don't ask for the assistance they could sorely do with; a misconception that strong independent people don't ask for help. Yet ironically, I bet you, like me, are always ready to lend a hand to someone who needs it! Data also proves that people who are connected to others, have lower rates of anxiety and higher self-esteem. Connectedness, a feeling of inclusion and belonging, boosts our wellbeing on physical, social and emotional level. It has been such a blessing to see Anna thrive with the right support. And I am grateful to my tribe of loyal supporters.

If you struggle with anxiety, finding someone you feel comfortable talking to, can make all the difference to your confidence and ability to manage your situation, whether that is a friend, a coach, or a professionally trained advisor. With stress and anxiety on the rise, improving mental health in times of uncertainty, is now more important than ever, especially since Covid-19 has thrown out so many challenges to us all. I think 2020 has made us all aware of our potential vulnerabilities and encouraged us to build social connections through online platforms; to be more empathetic and inclusive; to build community and wellbeing. As the new 'normal' reveals itself over 2021, I hope you and I both continue to reach out in support of those who may need it.

Secondly, this year reminded me that even at our lowest point, we really do have the strengths and courage within us, to face our fears and manage those difficult times. It's one of life's paradoxes that the worst situations have the ability to bring out the best in us. We just must remember to use these innate resources that we are blessed with; to stop worrying about what qualities we don't possess and recognise that we *do* have the power to change our lives, and those around us, for the better.

A bit about Grit

I first came across the term 'Grit' and the role it plays in our success, when I read Angela Duckworth's book *Grit: The Power of Passion and Perseverance*. I've seen *grit* defined as "firmness of character; indomitable spirit" which induced me to conjure up images of very tough, extraordinary men and women; war heroes perhaps, from a far-removed world of experiences than the likes of me. But actually, it's much simpler and attainable. *Grit* is about wanting to improve and succeed, the determination not to give up on something that matters to you, until you've completed what you set out to do; to stick it out even though it's hard, because it's important to you. Let's be honest, we've all had times when we've succeeded in life because we've wanted something badly enough, that we've stuck it out. Grit matters because it drives achievement and success. Every hurdle that we face gives us the opportunity to become stronger, more resilient and grittier.

Climbing back up on top

Not quite out of the firing line, I still faced more surgery and I am aware that I will continue to need medical intervention on both my ankles for the rest of my life. As long as I can continue to remain upright, I will do whatever is required to be done and I will never fail to be grateful that I have such incredible people fixing me and supporting me. Fortunately, this next operation was a small boost to help the pain and optimise movement. Hopefully it will keep me out of the operating theatre for at least another

18 months! I decided to ditch the heavy meds, as a consequence, and relied on acupuncture to relieve the residual nerve pain.

They say that every storm in your life is followed by a rainbow. Well, our storm had been a heavy one and our rainbow was bright.

The latter half of our year was filled with happiness and so welcome after a tough beginning: a wonderful holiday in Portugal, en famile; the joy of seeing both our children flourish; a beautiful family wedding; a dream trip to Zambia; an opportunity to co-facilitate training with a very dear friend, in Athens; everything culminating in a wonderful family reunion in Spain, for George's Graduation. Cadet to Pilot; our little boy's dream, now his adult reality. How proud we were to see him receive his Wings!

Our spirits were high and life felt good.

Chapter 9
CREATING HAPPINESS

So, what *is* happiness?

How would you describe happiness?

I resonate with how Sonja Lyubomirsky (Positive psychology researcher) describes it: "the experience of joy, contentment, or positive well-being, combined with a sense that one's life is good, meaningful and worthwhile".

I find it funny that we all can recall things that have made us happy but nobody knows what happiness feels like for others, we can only go by our own experience of it. What drives my vision of a happy life might seem utterly horrendous to you! Yet happiness, or lack of it, has a huge impact on the way we live our lives.

What does happiness mean to you?

Happiness for me is having a purpose, knowing my strengths and putting them to good use in many different ways.

And being by the sea. That's my happy place. Do you have one?

Have you noticed that as you get older, your concept of happiness evolves and mellows in line with your motivations and goals? Whilst I don't believe our inner child ever leaves us - I still love to have fun, enjoy learning and expanding my horizons, I notice that the almost giddy excitement and anticipation of what the future would bring, in my youth, is giving way to gratitude and fulfilment of what I've achieved and what I have.

The sad truth, however, is that in recent years, as a society, we have become richer but less happy. Stress and mental health issues are on the rise and have become a global concern. Wellbeing, particularly in the workplace, has become a necessary focus. There is a tendency to keep expecting more, focusing on what we lack, rather than savouring what we have, comparing our lives and successes to others and feeling discontented. Simple as this sounds, learning to be satisfied with what we have, can be surprisingly difficult. With progress comes a natural tendency for us to want more. Pressures though social media of seemingly perfect people, with perfect lives don't help, creating a false reality that drains happiness. Managing our own expectations is paramount to being happy and setting meaningful goals focused on our strengths, that provide us with structure and purpose, give us a sense of identity and increase our self-esteem.

How happy and content do you feel? On a scale of happiness, from 1 (miserable) - 10 (joyful and content), how would you rate yourself?

In pursuit of happiness

There is no doubt that we lose some of our spontaneous childhood joy as we grow up. Pressures of life cause us to become more contained, sceptical, stressed, fearful, judgemental in our outlook. I have heard happiness described as "something to look forward to", "something we work towards". People attach "*if*" and "*when*" to happiness – *"I'll be happy if I get my dream job"; "I'll be happy when I lose weight"*. Happiness becomes something elusive – a magical place in the future. But it doesn't need to be. I realised when I had my accident and couldn't do so many basic things, that in reality, happiness was – and is - each small win along my journey towards recovery, the joy of every good moment in my day. Learning to be thankful for the little blessings, even at those disappointing times when things aren't what I expect.

I remember a specific morning, following my last ankle surgery, I was, rather grumpily, hopping up the road on my crutches, ankle in a cast, irritated that my shoulder bag was getting in the way of my uneven gait and making my movement more awkward than necessary, when one of the local gardeners stopped me to say "madam, in my country when we have a fracture, we just take a rest. You are running fast on your two sticks with your broken leg". It made me laugh out loud; 'running' I was not - but it reminded me that despite the pain and inconvenience, how truly appreciative I was to be able to get outdoors, be active and independent; how very lucky I am, under the circumstances, that I have both my feet and am able to walk! And with it, was the realisation that *it's not about the happy ending, but our story along the way.* There is no need to postpone happiness.

What are you thankful for?

What makes your heart sing?

The science of happiness

When it comes to happiness, research reveals:

- 50% is in your genetic makeup - admittedly you don't have control over this but if your parents are happy people, you have a natural advantage.

- 40% is in your power to control!

- 10% is circumstantial - so whether you win the lottery, or like me, have a terrible accident, it should not impact your happiness by more than 10%!

So, happiness is more about our mindset than our circumstances, and much of that is down to *us* to make happen. *We* give our lives meaning. We can't change our genes but we can change ourselves. Happiness is something we choose.

Of course, it would be completely unrealistic to feel chirpy all the time. As I mentioned earlier, negative emotions are instinctive when we encounter adversity, in a bid to prepare us for action and keep us "safe" and it would be foolhardy not to acknowledge them. Negative thinking happens to us all. Whether you have suffered catastrophic loss in your life or not, we all go through times when we feel stressed and overwhelmed, when feeling joyful is not exactly at the front of mind. Happiness is making the most of the good times and coping with the inevitable difficult times, managing those negative thinking traps and our harsh inner critic. By doing so we are taking a big step towards a happier life.

You may wonder: *What's so great about happiness, anyway?*

Well, the scientific evidence for happiness is compelling. Happiness is not a fluffy luxury for a select few. According to behavioural scientists, happiness leads to a wide range of benefits for our performance, relationships and wellbeing in life. Science proves that happy people have better overall health and live longer than their less happy peers. Happy people thrive.

Who would really choose to skip cheerily and readily into pain and loss? And why would any of us want to do more of what makes us unhappy?

None of us would deliberately seek out a life of misery. Positive influences make our lives fulfilling. The key to being happy is to recognise that you have the power to decide what to accept and what to let go. So, rather than success being the means to our happiness, research shows that happiness could, in fact, be the source of our success.

Gratitude – the parent of all virtues

"Gratitude is not only the greatest of virtues but the parent of all the others". Cicero (Roman Orator)

Just a smidgen more to champion *Gratitude*. Study after study continues to reveal a strong association between gratitude and wellbeing, better mental health, more fulfilling relationships, greater optimism and higher resilience. A little reminder to practice the simple daily exercise: *The Three Good Things*!

You have the power to control how fulfilling your life is. Writing down the things that give your life meaning, increase your wellbeing and bring happiness, helps to strengthen those concepts in your mind. Not only does writing mine make me feel happier, I hope I can also serve to inspire you to create more of what makes you happy.

Embracing kindness

Can you remember how you felt when a random stranger was kind to you?

Only yesterday, I dropped my car key whilst trying to transport too many groceries at one time and, typically, it fell under the car. Exasperated, I started to put down my shopping to look for it when a little boy, not more than 6 or 7 years old, walking out of the shop with his mother, raced across the pavement, crawled under the car and handed the key to me, with a big smile on his face. What a sweetie! It put a smile on my face! His mother was, quite understandably, most proud of him.

Perhaps you can recall the last time you were kind to someone? I really try hard to be kind. It is a value that my parents instilled in me and, as a natural chatter box (I talk with everyone!), there's no doubt that it does make me feel good to brighten someone's day.

Science proves that generous behaviour increases your instances of being happy. It lowers your stress levels and helps build relationship bonds. Kindness doesn't need to be anything elaborate or expensive. It is not something that demands hard work or has to take up masses of your time but carrying out a kind act for others, releases your feel-good hormones (endorphins and oxytocin) and has a multiplier effect – by making a conscious effort to put a smile on someone else's face it, in turn, makes you feel good. It's a win-win situation!

Researchers have found that being kind to ourselves, to others, or actively observing kindness around us, boosts our happiness.

Being kind is a choice that we can make every day. It's not about seeking credit or a wide audience. We shouldn't expect a payback.

I remember a lovely guy, Brian, who worked in our company – those of you who have worked with me, will recall this story, I'm sure. He stopped during one morning on his way to the office, to get petrol. It was a sweltering summer day and sweat was pouring down the faces of the attendants working outside. Whilst they were filling his car, he went into the little shop and purchased ice-creams for all of them. He hadn't done it to be noticed but someone saw him and phoned in to the morning radio show and shared the story. Brian was amazed when it was repeated during our morning Huddle in the office. I just think that that was such a beautiful act of kindness hence the reason I have never forgotten the story. I think we can all learn from that.

Kindness is lasting. How do you want to be remembered?

Hope - our fuel for living

If gratitude is appreciating what we have and happiness is savouring the present good, hope is envisioning a valued future. Our belief that something positive will come from a difficult situation.

If you can face the hurdles thrown at you, feeling that there is something you can do about them, your life will become easier to live. Hope is that catalyst. It motivates us to attain an outcome that we would like to see. Without hope, I've seen people lose their motivation to keep going because they can't see an end to obstacles that appear uncompromising. I find that heart-breaking.

I know that when things come crashing around our ears, it's not easy to feel hopeful. But hope doesn't mean everything will be amazing. It's not about wishful thinking or deluding yourself that everything will be just fine. Like optimism, it is a realistic expectation that there are possibilities and that something good can come of the troubles you're facing. Hope strengthens your determination and persistence to find the right pathways to your goals. It's being able to envision what you want and look for different routes to achieve it.

I survived my terrible trauma because I had, and continue to have, hope. Being hopeful enables me to focus on my next goal when adversity strikes. It has built my resilience. I don't allow my negative circumstances to restrict who I am and how I can live my life. I am not pain free and live with constant discomfort; restricted movement that continues to challenge my medical team, but whilst I am aware that it will never be entirely resolved, I have great hope that evolving medical technology will enable me to continue to live a full, productive and happy life, despite it all. I will continue to make progress, whichever direction it may take.

Hope is our bedrock. Hope is our energy for life. And it is a key factor in promoting our happiness. Getting your hopes up in miserable situations always feels good.

Everything you do either contributes to, or takes away from, living a hopeful, happy life.

How do you create hope for yourself and how do you support hope in others?

We may not be able to control our future but we can imagine a better one and takes steps to make it happen.

Carpe Diem – seize the day

We all have the ability to make small changes in our behaviour, our relationships and the context in which we live, which can put us firmly on track for a happier life.

Here are my key criteria for happiness:

- **Don't wait to be happy. Choose happiness first.**

- **Look at what is right in your life; don't focus on what is wrong** (if you look for a problem, you will always find one).

- A Persian proverb *"I cried because I had no shoes, until I met a man with no feet"*. **Appreciate what you have.**

- **Notice what makes you happy.** When you've had the *best* day, what made it so great? When you are aware of the things that make you happy, find ways to do more of them. Figure out what makes you unhappy and avoid those things, or people, as far as possible!

- **Don't compare yourself to others**. There's a saying: *Life is the most difficult exam. Many people fail because they try to copy others, not realising that everyone has a different question paper.* We each have our own unique set of strengths and we each have a unique journey.

- And take social media with a big pinch of salt – no-one is going to be posting their failures and flaunting their low points. No-one leads a perfect life.

- **Let go of resentment.** It only serves to increase your bitterness.

- **Be kind to yourself.** When you feel low, imagine what advice you would offer a friend in that situation and then apply that to yourself.

- **Know your strengths and put them to good use.** Find your flow.

Happiness is a combination of many different things, unique to each of us, but overall, it's the satisfying feeling that your life is well lived.

I am reminded of my friend's favourite quote by John Lennon: *"When I was 5 years old, my mother always told me that happiness was the key to life. When I went to school, they asked me what I wanted to be when I grew up. I wrote down 'happy'. They told me I didn't understand the assignment and I told them they didn't understand life".*

What are your essential ingredients for happiness? What changes do you need to make, to feel you are living your life in the happiest way?

Chapter 10
THE CHOICES WE MAKE

"You may not control all the events that happen to you, but you can decide not to be reduced by them". **Maya Angelou**

Have you ever achieved anything of value without encountering some sort of challenge?

When I was a little girl, living in Africa, we used to go often to the beach and were lucky to have many choices along the coast. Some of the beaches were gorgeous but the sea was rough; huge waves crashing onto the shore, with a swift undercurrent that could knock you off balance as you stood ankle deep in the water. Often beyond the shoreline, the sea was less boisterous but getting past that initial barricade was scary. If you waited long enough, there was often a small window of opportunity, when the waves subsided enough for you to quickly slide into the sea and reach the calmer water beyond. It was a safe option but you couldn't be sure how long you'd have to wait. I decided that it was more effective to bite the bullet, to dive straight into those intimidating waves and swim beyond the turbulence fast. Actually, it wasn't as difficult as one thought and once you were in, the sea was glorious. I think this has always been my approach to challenges. Meeting the difficulty head on, being relentless, being determined and, most importantly, having the belief that I *will* get through it and things *will* be ok.

Have you ever backed down from a goal because the challenge or setback seemed overwhelming at the time? What was it that stopped you? Reflecting on that situation now, might there have been a way to push forwards which you deliberately ignored, or perhaps didn't think of?

Life presents us with an infinite number of choices. There are no guarantees that the choices you make are going to give you the outcome you seek and there are times you may feel powerless because many things may be outside your control. You have the choice though, of closing down and feeling lost, or you can take charge of your situation. Your choice defines your experience.

When life kicks you down, it does not have to determine the outcome of your life. You can elect to see all the problems, to focus on what's wrong, or you can choose to reflect on what is going right and the opportunities in front of you. *You determine your route, nobody else.*

It is said that we have to do hard things to grow but success in life is not an accident. It takes effort. I've learned that change is necessary - and possible. And that if I make choices that don't help me, I can make different choices – and, believe me, I have had to do that many times until I reach the outcome I want to see! But I believe that we can reinvent ourselves at any time. We have all the personal resources we need; the ability to touch excellence and achieve extraordinary things. Success doesn't mean an absence of problems, but each obstacle we face shapes us and offers us the opportunity to learn from it – let's be honest, challenges force us to experience and manage things we may never have been exposed to, if we had the choice of 'playing it safe'. These difficulties, like them or not, help us discover our strengths. This is how we develop resilience. To be at our best we have to keep evolving, in order to flourish.

What's key is to recognise that *you always have control of what you do next*. Even in the darkest, most challenging of circumstances, you still have the choice of how you see that situation and how you choose to respond. Your success in everything you undertake, is a result of your mindset and your attitude is your choice.

"In times of adversity and change we really discover who we are and what we're made up of". Howard Schultz

Having experienced so many hurdles since my accident seven years ago, on my long journey towards recovery, it has made me appreciate life in different ways.

The things that have challenged me most – sometimes to the extreme, have highlighted my vulnerabilities and in doing so, helped me to recognise my personal power, enabled me to use my strengths to achieve things I didn't think possible. I have a deeper understanding of who I am and what I am capable of. Resilience is empowering.

Whilst I'm still a work in progress, these testing experiences have enabled me to clarify my purpose and what matters most to me and empowered me to focus on where I can create meaning and impact, to enable others to flourish.

If these last few years have taught me anything about life, it's that it's fragile. I re-emphasise, there are no guarantees and no promise that what we can do today will be a certainty tomorrow. Health, wealth, wellbeing, career, loved ones...We mustn't take for granted all the blessings we have around us, for in a short moment, everything can change. "Life's too short" is something I've heard said so many times and yet too many people continue to sweat the small stuff, fail to make the changes they would like to see. Instead worry, fears and judgemental comparisons unhelpfully stand in the way, keeping happiness at bay.

I don't want to just exist, I want to feel that I'm living my life with purpose and I've learned that no matter what the universe hurls at you, however dire your situation, you *can* choose optimism, find meaning, hope and happiness. I appreciate everything that brings joy into my life, so much more.

"Don't let the bugger break you down"

I remember my Mother-in-Law telling me this many years ago. It made me laugh, it made me determined not to allow people or circumstances to demoralise me and it is a mantra I use if I feel my courage slipping.

I never want to look back with regret, feeling that I didn't take the chance to do something I wanted, because it scared me. So, despite my huge personal challenges, I decided to take a leap of faith this last year and move out of the corporate world that I had been a part of for 30 years! A scary but liberating decision and one of the best I have ever made! I set up my own professional development company, focusing individuals and organisations on their unique value to the world. Enabling them, through strengths-based development, to harness their potential and transform what is good, into something superb. During this difficult time in the world, so many people and businesses have struggled and I have had the privilege of helping so many, move forwards. As a Master of Resilience, I was delighted to have been invited onto Dubai One TV and interviewed in different parts of the globe (courtesy of online platforms!), to share insights on how to thrive through disruption and raise wellbeing during remote working. I am living my purpose and I feel so fulfilled by enabling others to flourish.

I can't predict what the future will hold, though I know it will involve further trips to the Operating Theatre, but I have chosen to maximise my life and that means looking beyond the adversity and knowing that I *will* make the most of my circumstances, whatever they might be.

How satisfied do you feel with your life? What part of it needs a boost? What choices will you make to enable you to live your *best* life?

You may have your own list of the things in life that help you thrive but I'd like to share my suggestions, based on my experiences.

- **Be your authentic self**. Understand your unique strengths. You are special and so is the value you bring to the world.

- **Treasure your family and the good people around you** who, in their different ways, enrich your life.

- **Learn to expect more from life**. As Steve Jobs said: "*If you haven't found it yet, keep looking. Don't settle*". Life always has more to give. Figure out what's important to you and don't forfeit your vision.

- **Choose courage over fear.** You are stronger than you think. Don't live with regret.

- **Find your purpose**. Remember we are all here to put our dent in the universe. What do you want to be known for? Find your passion and love what you do.

- **Take action.** All your greatest ideas are only a pipe dream until you make them your reality. Your *Circle of Influence* empowers you to make necessary changes you would like to see.

- **Don't underestimate your ability to thrive**. You are much stronger that you think.

Whether we like it or not, adversity is part of life. You and I may face unique challenging experiences but we learn similar lessons, and when our world falls apart, we both have all the resources we need to come prepared for each challenge, to overcome those difficulties and to pass this test of life.

"When you are in a dark place, you sometimes tend to think that you've been buried. Perhaps you've been planted. Bloom."

Don't settle for a smaller life than you are capable of living. Hang in there. Have faith. Choose to flourish.

TOOLKIT FOR FLOURISHING

1. **MINDSET MATTERS; TAKING CONTROL**

2. **A GLASS HALF FULL**

3. **KNOWING YOUR PURPOSE**

1
MINDSET MATTERS; TAKING CONTROL

Your success and happiness depend on your frame of mind

None of us can progress through life successfully dodging every difficult situation. Your mindset plays a critical role in how you cope when challenges come hurtling at you. Even if you are naturally confident, when you're facing major obstacles, it can create self-doubt and cause you to question your personal competence. When you feel stressed and drained, it can suck you into a downward spiral of negative thoughts and unhappy feelings which cloud your vision and make your situation feel even worse.

Since mindset has a major effect on how we learn, perform and grow, I thought I'd share with you a bit of neuroscience to explain why we think as we do, and some strategies which I learned that I have found particularly helpful. They enable me to question my negative thoughts and any underlying assumptions I have, so I can review my situation more rationally. This ensures that I focus on opportunities, rather than disasters, when I feel stuck. Not only has this improved my resilience, I find this to be a great stress buster because I feel more confident in the choices I make. I hope it helps you, too.

Our lens of the world

As I have explained, what you tell yourself is what you believe - your thoughts create your reality. You *do* become what you most often think about, so you need to watch what you are feeding your mind.

This Cognitive Model image below, represents the relationship between the world and how we feel.

Cognitive Model

Simply explained:

Our thoughts, feelings and behaviours are connected.

We each see the world through our unique lens, based on our life experiences, beliefs and values.

When something happens, we interpret that event with series of thoughts, beliefs and ideas (our inner dialogue) and give it a conscious meaning. This results in us feeling a certain way and encourages us to act in response to that feeling.

Our core beliefs influence 95% of the decisions we make and the actions we take accordingly.

Unfortunately, we are innately wired to pay more attention to negative events than positive ones (a survival instinct to protect ourselves). We fall into familiar ways of thinking and can get trapped into visualizing just one way to do things. What we do or say can become engrained in our brain as habits. Ninety percent of all our thoughts are repetitive, so if our negative thoughts get repeated enough, they become habitual. When we get too fixed in our thinking, we become less able to look at a situation clearly and we make errors of judgement. This tendency is exacerbated when we feel stressed as our negative thoughts influence our emotions and distort our perception of reality. Our brains can work overtime developing worse case scenarios!

These unhelpful thoughts and language can trap you in anxiety, self-doubt, anger and depression, get in the way of problem solving and are the easiest way to slow down your personal and business progress.

The good news is that you don't need to resign yourself to living with these counterproductive thought patterns; you can break this negative thinking cycle, change your mood and modify your behaviour, so that you take back control of your situation.

Developing healthier thinking

Mental agility is a skill which helps you to see things from different perspectives, so that you can meet your stressful situations head on and decide on the best action to move forward effectively. This skill takes practice but the more you do, you will notice that you are changing the tone of your thoughts from negative to positive which serve to help you, rather than trip you up.

The strategies I am sharing below, will help you to better understand your unhelpful thoughts and enable you to practice resilient responses, so you are better equipped for when the next challenge arises. You can apply the framework below to any situation where you feel stuck.

Everything begins with the thoughts you pay attention to, so focus on what you want to attract into your life.

How to tame self-defeating thinking

Self-awareness activity

This activity will help you with the following:

- identify the negative thoughts that cause you to make inaccurate assumptions and understand what underlying beliefs are behind them.

- learn to challenge these distortive thoughts and reframe them with a fairer, more balanced perspective.

- create actionable steps to manage them, rather than let them manage you.

Do grab a pen and paper and when you are ready to start, begin by generating a situation that triggers you to catastrophize.

Apply the following approaches to that situation. Make note of your reactions, as you work through each section, so you are very clear on what negative thoughts are getting in your way. Then, create new, more effective responses, so you can visualise a more successful outcome to that situation.

I. Identify what pushes your buttons

What triggered you to feel negatively? Was it a situation? A person? A bad memory of a past experience?

- Make a note of what each of those triggers were, so you get clarity and remember them for future awareness.

- Gauge the severity their impact on your thinking by identifying what level of distress that trigger initiated, on a scale of 1 (minor irritation) to 10 (extreme distress).

- Ask yourself why you felt threatened in that situation. How did you react? Note that your biggest strengths can be your biggest weakness, when they are neglected, overused or frustrated, they cause us to react unreasonably.

II. **What stories are you telling yourself?**

Our reaction to anything, is based on the subjective perception we have about that specific thing. This allows us to label it accordingly: threat or safe, bad or good? Our stories can empower or derail us. Feelings are not facts but we can allow them to spin narratives about the likely outcome of our experience and often they are wide off the mark. Our inner critic can be hurtful and the stories we tell ourselves can turn into deeply held personal beliefs, so you need to monitor your inner dialogue and understand what it's telling you.

- Think about what caused your situation to happen. Describe the event to yourself as accurately as you can. What does that event say about you? How did it affect the people or situation around you?

- Notice when you are being self-critical. What are you telling yourself? Are there key phrases that you use? What tone do you take with yourself – harsh? Angry? Impatient?

- Write down some of the negative statements you have had about yourself recently (eg: *I'm so fat; If I don't accomplish X, I will never be worthy of Y; I'm a failure and nobody likes me*).

- Now distinguish between what is a fact and what is your opinion. Your opinion can be misleading. Ask yourself: *Is that opinion justified?* It's important to evaluate facts and opinions carefully in order to draw the right conclusions

III. Rewind the story. Separate yourself from your inner critic.

- Ask yourself: *What was upsetting me in that story scenario? Is this thought helpful or making my situation worse? Is my interpretation fair? Is there a different way to see it? What other choices are there? Could I have done something better? What's the most positive interpretation of this that I can think of?* Stories are created by the meaning we give them.

- Look at your story objectively. Change the statements that run through your head into questions, based on the above, and then focus your thoughts on finding answers to those questions.

- Rewrite your script. A compassionate view would be to ask yourself: what would I say to my best friend in this situation?

IV. Be mindful of your thinking traps. Our brain is constantly trying to interpret and make sense of the world around us. Sometimes it takes short cuts and makes inaccurate connections that prevent us from seeing things the way they really are. These thinking patterns are known as cognitive distortions. Whilst these counteractive thoughts are a part of life, if you give power to them, they cause you to make errors of judgment by twisting your thoughts and triggering feelings of negativity and pessimism.

Listed below are 10 common thinking traps. Generate some thoughts about conflicts you have faced recently. Which thinking traps do you notice that you struggle with?

1. **All-or-nothing thinking (black-and-white thinking**) You see a situation in extremes - either good or bad, success or failure – there is no middle ground and if you fall short of your expectations, you view yourself as a total failure.

2. **Catastrophising** You exaggerate the consequences of the negative things that happen to you, imagine the worst-case scenarios and predict that you won't be able to cope with them, which blocks you from taking action.

3. **Magnification/minimisation** When you evaluate yourself, another person, or a situation, you unreasonably magnify the negative aspects and minimize the positive aspects until they look insignificant.

4. **Mind reading** (otherwise known as projection): You believe you know what others are thinking and assume they are thinking the worst of you.

5. **Ruminating**: repetitively dwelling on every possible aspect of a problem and consequence – allowing it to go round and round your head.

6. **Personalisation:** You believe others are behaving negatively because of something you've said, or done, without considering more

plausible explanations for their behavior; you wrongfully assume responsibility

7. **Labelling:** You attach a negative label to yourself (or others), seeing a mistake or undesirable situation as defining who you are rather than a single event e.g. *I am a failure* vs *I failed this time*

8. **"Should" and "must" statements:** You have a precise, fixed idea of how you or others should behave, and you overestimate how bad it is if these expectations are not met.

9. **Filtering or tunnel vision**: You only see negative aspects of a situation and ignore all the positives.

10. **Being Right:** You go to any length to prove that your opinions and actions are the correct ones and that others are wrong.

Do any of these sound familiar to you? Keep a track of your thinking traps; get clear on which ones catch you out and why.

V. 3 steps to reframe your counterproductive thoughts

This enables you to neutralise your situational emotions and act more rationally.

Step 1: Challenge: Question your negative assumptions:

- *Is this thought helpful?*

- *Is it accurate?*

- *What other explanations are there?*

- Reflect on the worst-case scenario. What does that look like? (stressful!)

- Consider the best-case scenario. What does that look like? (hopeful!)

- Consider a purposeful outcome - what could I do in this situation?

(Usually, the outcome you are most likely to see will fall somewhere between the worst and best case and will bring your fearful thoughts to a more realistic level).

Step 2: Provide Evidence

Note the following:

The *'Pros'* which objectively support your thought: *e.g. When I did X, Y happened*

The *'Cons'* which objectively contradict your thought: e.g. *That's not true because...*

Step 3: Reframe: Put a more positive spin on it.

Reshape your story by telling yourself: *A better way to see this is...*

Changing the way in which you look at a situation will change your experience of it. Most stressful instances call for a more "moderate" explanation and by altering your perception of what is upsetting you, you can convert what seemed a highly traumatic event, into something you can overcome.

VI. **Plan:** Create a new habit - forget big changes and concentrate on tiny steps:

i. **If THIS happens**...   *identify the trigger*

ii. **Instead of doing...X**   *be clear on the behaviour you want to change*

iii. **I will do... Y**   *identify an easy quick win*

In his book *Rewire Your Brain*, John Arden (psychologist) states: *"The more you do something, the more likely it is that you will do it again in the future. Repetition rewires the brain and breeds habits. The more the neurons fire together, the more likely it is that they will fire together in the future"*.

What action plan will you put in motion?

Combat stressful situations ahead of time:

You can use these resilience skills preventatively. Get used to noticing when you are slipping into negative, stress-inducing spirals of thought. Practice challenging those unhelpful beliefs. Have some positive responses ready. Generating these positive feelings builds on your natural strengths, enables you to manage stress and create lasting change.

Practice real-time resilience:

Try this!

Challenge those counterproductive thoughts as they occur.

When you get caught up in the moment, say *STOP* out loud! It consciously interrupts your thoughts and allows you to reset your thinking.

Then you can respond to those negative thoughts by providing evidence and generating a more optimistic way of seeing it.

Name it to tame it

Psychologist Dr Dan Siegel used this expression to explain the importance of noticing and naming our emotion. Research proves that when you label difficult emotions, it reduces their hold over you. It also gives you a deeper understanding of what happened and how it affects you, which helps you see possibilities of what to do next. It is often harder than you think identifying exactly what you're feeling, especially if you are going through an emotional upheaval. But if someone asks you how you're doing, how often have you replied: *fine... ok ...good thanks,* or possibly, *a bit down*? These most obvious labels that we resort to are pretty vague descriptors. They are not going to help. Putting feelings into words actually takes practice. When you feel that you are becoming tense and upset, try to attach a word that describes your experience.

Say that again

You talk to yourself more than you talk to anyone else and that little voice in your head has plenty to tell you; interpreting, explaining and judging everything you encounter. When you are in a challenging situation, the words you use in that particular conversation with yourself, will determine how long you will be stuck in that position. Some words suggest defeat before you start. Here are some well-known success stoppers that you will recognise and suggestions for a better outcome:

- *I can't*: end of story! Is it really impossible, or you don't want to? Instead: *How can I?*

- *I'll try to*: a get out clause, non-committal!

  Instead: *I will ..I am.. I have*

- *Always / Never*: is that a fact? Avoid absolutes.

  Instead: *Occasionally, sometimes*

- *Good*: self-limiting

  Instead: *Excellent; awesome!*

What words do you notice that you use which can be self-defeating? Your language impacts how others perceive and relate to you. If you feel overlooked and undervalued, for example, could it be that you are talking yourself down and undermining your own authority and power? Positive, action focused words inspire trust and confidence. What you picture in your mind when you use certain words is crucial to how you interpret them and their impact on you. For example: *Don't panic* vs *I can do this*.

Did you know? Saying "*I choose*" is a highly effective option because it changes your beliefs and your power in a situation.

As Tony Robbins wisely recommends: "*If we want to change our lives and shape our destiny, we need to consciously select the words we're going to use and need to constantly strive to expand our level of choices*".

What remains unconscious will continue to have control over you. Getting to understand your own mind takes time but the results are so worth the effort once you develop the habit of practicing these skills. Of course, none of us are perfect and, despite our best efforts, we don't get it right every time, but those limiting beliefs are self-sabotaging, so the sooner you can get to grips with them, the better. You are the only person who can initiate those changes. If you feel discouraged just remember you have successfully managed stressful situations in the past. Bring to mind previous experiences where you navigated those difficult situations and note what you did. How can you recreate more of those positive outcomes? Use your own successes to give yourself hope that you can get through other challenges, too. Remember, what you pay attention to will shape your experiences. Don't allow negative thoughts to write the story of those experiences. What you tell yourself matters.

2
A GLASS HALF FULL

How do you define your setbacks?

Let's face it, we all feel pressure and encounter problems that can stress us out. When you're facing a roadblock, how do you talk to yourself about it?

When it comes to enduring challenges, your resilience depends on the way you explain your situation to yourself and how you respond to that challenge.

Responding to challenges with optimism

Think of two or three specific events recently, when your day was shaken up. Maybe you want to grab a pen and write them down. When you unravel those situations, what did your mind land on? What went wrong and stressed you out? Or what you did to set it to rights?

I think we've all been asked at some point whether we see our metaphorical "glass" as *half full* or *half empty*. How do you see yours? Most people tend to lean towards one of these mindsets more than the other. I must come clean here, I am a natural optimist. I believe that things *will* work out. My glass is always half full. I read an article once that described optimism as a 'Get Out of Jail Free' card. I love that idea. That's how I think of optimism; it frees your mind so you can move forwards with hope and motivation.

However, contrary to some thinking, optimism is not about having a "Pollyanna" approach, with the assumption that optimists only see the positive in every situation. It's simply not true. Optimists are not naïve but they have a natural conviction that when things get tough, they will cope. The real difference between realistic optimists and pessimists isn't in their level of happiness but in how they *weather their storms*.

Seven years down the line, the issues with my ankles manifest itself in pain, a constrictive tightness around my left ankle which limits movement and makes my gait awkward, and which often results in cramps in my leg and feet at night. I have constant buzzing of 'pins and needles' in both feet, from nerve damage, and the metalwork in my right lower leg grates on my ankle bone. I know that much of this damage is permanent and for the most part, I accept I must live with it. I know that I will need more surgery moving forwards and I rely on modern medicine to keep me out of a wheelchair permanently. But rather than see endless problems, being optimistic enables me to look at what I can do to make my situation better. Whilst I'm bitterly disappointed that I can never run again, I have found other sport and exercise that I can do every day, which keeps me mentally sane and fit. As I mentioned, I have a passion for Doc Martens and now I have a great collection to wear. I have found a brilliant surgeon who gives me hope of future possibilities. With the worst-case scenario in mind, I have faced the thought of amputation and know that if it ever came to that, I have the strengths and resources to cope and not allow it to make my life smaller.

There is no doubt that I see and feel the limitations each time I get knocked back. It hurts physically and mentally but whilst I might despair briefly, I explain rubbish situations to myself as challenges, not all-consuming threats on my life. I've found that being optimistic helps me cope better when I'm feeling depleted or run down. Acceptance can be quite liberating. I don't believe that just because I have a positive mindset, good things will just appear but having that positive energy, I believe I have the ability to control much of my destiny and so I tend to meet things head on, focus on what I can do, in my *Circle of Influence*, and I act accordingly. And this helps me recover from disappointments more quickly.

I think feeling in control of your circumstance really matters. I firmly believe I can *always* take some positive action in an adverse situation which makes my life better. I believe we all can. If you take a passive approach because you feel that your future is hopeless and everything you do is wrong, you will always feel stuck in victim zone and that's a debilitating place to be. It makes you afraid of new experiences, of uncertainty, and it eats away at your self-confidence.

There are tangible effects to looking on the bright side. Science proves that how we perceive and respond to events and challenges in our lives, matters for our happiness and health. Decades of research confirms that an optimistic mindset promotes better overall health and a longer life. Like resilience, optimism is partly down to your genes but, again, like resilience, anyone can learn how to adopt an optimistic mindset.

You, like me, may be an optimist but there is no magic bullet! Optimism is your belief system, your set of thoughts, that drives the way you think, feel and behave. If, however, your glass is looking 'half empty' and you would like to see that glass 'half full' - and perhaps, with a dash of soda and a clink of ice – let's look at a few tactics to make that happen.

1. **Evaluate your optimism**

There are 2 key ways to assess optimism:

1. Dispositional: your tendency to expect good outcomes across all areas of your life, even in uncertain times.

2. Your explanatory style: how you explain to yourself the causes of good and bad news. *Marty Seligman's* ("Founder" of Positive Psychology) concept of the 3P's, below, helps in making sense of your experiences.

Do read through the following statements and consider what your natural reaction is.

What do identify about yourself?

- **Personalisation:** *"It's ME!"*

   Your fault, or circumstance?

   Pessimists take disappointments and rejections personally, blaming themselves for any failure or setback in their lives, whereas optimists accept that not everything that happens to them, happens because of them, and that the likelihood is that next time, that situation may have a better outcome.

   At the same time, interestingly, optimists tend to view good events as being a result of their own efforts, while pessimists link good outcomes to external influences.

- **Permanence**: *"It will last forever!"*

   Temporary, or everlasting?

   Optimists tend to view bad times as a temporary setback; a challenge that can be overcome or fixed. Pessimists are more likely to see negative events as permanent and unchangeable. Therefore, they are more likely to feel helpless in the face of failure and feel like giving up when things get tough.

- **Pervasiveness**: *"It will affect everything I do!"*

Specific, or all inclusive?

When optimists experience failure in one area of their life, they don't let it influence their beliefs about their abilities in other areas. They also allow a happy occurrence to brighten up every area of their lives rather than attribute it to just one experience. Pessimists, however, assume that failure in one area means that their whole life is likely to be doomed.

In conclusion: Optimism goes hand in hand with action. Life is not rosy but expecting good things to happen, will lead you to take actions that make your situation better. Pessimism can close your mind to opportunities. If you expect to lurch from crisis to crisis, you'll get stuck focusing on what else could go wrong and that will prevent you from doing the very things that might have minimised or prevented it from happening.

Stressful situations are created, in part, by the negative statements we tell ourselves. In every miserable experience you can still find a meaningful opportunity, if you look for it...*what can I learn from this? Is there anything I can be grateful for? What can I do differently that might help me?* By challenging and reframing your explanation, it does give you a more balanced perspective and a more hopeful outlook.

Take a few moments to bring to mind a difficult situation you're trying to cope with. Evaluate the way in which you're describing the adversity in your story. Have a go at reconstructing that story using the above concept of the 3P's. Is there another perspective in which to see it?

2. **Adjust your lens**

If you habitually tend to view things as negative, try reframing it in a positive light.

For example: in the recent months of global disruption, remote working and social distancing, I asked my clients, that apart from the many challenging things they all had to deal with, to focus on what they actually gained during this time. Responses have included: more time with their family, time for self-reflection and self-development, learning new skills, reading more books, becoming more health conscious, building better connections with family and friends and colleagues.

What rays of hope can you focus on?

Notice when good things happen. By making a conscious effort to look through a positive lens, it shifts your viewpoint and reframes your perspective. And as I explain in more detail in the section: *A Positive Approach*, conjuring up positive images and emotions, over time, trains your brain to automatically reach for positive responses over negative experiences.

Believe that you can make good things happen in your life. Practice pointing out to yourself where you have succeeded and how you achieved it. Think of other specific things you can do to succeed. e.g. *If I develop my understanding of my strengths and know what makes me stand out, I can focus on becoming an expert in my field.* And when something good happens to you, give yourself credit. How did you effect that good outcome? Be your own cheerleader!

3. Learn to let go

Don't cling on to something that is not serving you a helpful purpose. Holding on to negative emotions is draining and toxic. Be mindful of your thinking traps and inner dialogue. Deliberately shift your focus to something positive – look for the silver lining – even if it seems impossible, there is always one, even in the darkest of situations.

4. Keep the right company

I'm sure you can think of at least one person you know who complains all the time and /or is a naughty gossip. You may know someone who puts you down, makes you feel small, undermines your confidence. Negativity is contagious! It's emotionally draining and drags you down. Positivity is contagious, too, but it lifts you up and carries you high. Take some time to think about who you spend your time with. Are you surrounding yourself with the right people?

5. Be kind to yourself

We can put so much pressure on ourselves to be all things to all people: to be a good life partner, a good parent, a supportive family member, a worthy leader, colleague, friend... We compare ourselves to others, we judge them and we judge ourselves. We commit to working harder, for longer. We can be harsh on ourselves when things don't go our way. If you can relate to any of these, cut yourself some slack! Take some time for self-care. When you are less tired and less anxious you make better decisions, feel more resilient, are more productive and have happier relationships.

6. Practice gratitude

I definitely associate gratitude with greater happiness. When I conjure up images of things that have gone right in my day and acknowledge who, or what, was responsible for that, I can't help but feel a rush of positive emotion when I savour those good experiences. I've learned that gratitude makes you more energetic and optimistic. Certainly, research proves that counting your blessings is good for your health, boosts your self-worth and self-confidence, reduces stress, helps you become more resilient and builds stronger relationships. How do you capture the good events in your life? What are you most grateful for?

Whether or not, like me, you see your glass 'half full', you have the choice every day to decide how full or how empty your glass is. Your perspective of a setback can have a huge impact on your success and happiness. Don't allow your negative thoughts to become a self-fulfilling prophecy. My advice is to believe that good times will always come however rough today might be. After all, if your glass gets spilt, you can always refill it – fuller – and with a cocktail cherry on the side.

3
KNOWING YOUR PURPOSE

"What's the why behind everything you do? When we know this in life or design it, it is very empowering and the path is clear." Jack Canfield

Some days our biggest leap of faith is to get out of bed in the morning. Have you had days when you've just wondered what on earth is the point of your life? When it takes everything you've got to get up and just put one foot in front of the other? I've had several days over the years, when I felt this way.

I've learned that at times like these, knowing your purpose, your direction...your reason for being, is your lifeline. Feeling that your life is valuable, that you can create a positive impact.

If you are familiar with Simon Sinek (author and motivational speaker), he refers to this purpose as our WHY. The Japanese concept is known as Ikigai, roughly translated as "the thing that you live for". Others describe it as our Emotionally Charged Connection. It doesn't matter what name you give it but it is the reason you do what you do. It is what gives your life meaning.

When did you last think about your purpose?

Do you ever wonder why you do what you do?

Do you know your purpose in life?

A transformative realisation!

Honestly, I hadn't given this a lot of conscious deliberation until the question was posed to me.

Shortly after my Dad died, one of our friends, Charlie, unexpectedly died, too. Still reeling from losing my Dad, this was another shock. Another person gone too soon. And still with so much life in front of him. Or so we thought. It was a such a sad time. We held a celebration of Charlie's life, at our villa and it was a beautiful, rather spiritual, afternoon.

As we were pondering the journey of life, one of Charlie's friends asked me: "What do you think was the point of your accident?" His question threw me because I had never contemplated that before. It really made me think and I contemplated that question for days after. When I thought of my Dad and Charlie, taken from us so unexpectedly, I believe there must have been a reason why I survived such a big trauma. *Why* wasn't very obvious at first. I realised that I was actually just *existing* - coasting; getting over each hurdle, most definitely, but on autopilot mode. I knew I was resilient but wasn't consciously aware of what I was doing or why.

What was driving me? I started by getting clear on what I was actually doing, and how, and I realised that each time I was knocked back, I was instinctively tapping into reserves of energy, determination and courage that I didn't know I had – my innate "toolkit" of resources – which enabled me to focus and get back on track. And, for the most part, I wasn't just surviving, I was learning to thrive. And the more challenges I had to face, the better at this I became.

Wherever purpose goes, meaning wants to follow "*Why* do I do what I do?" It's impossible to answer that question accurately, without identifying what your "work" actually is. Get clear on your purpose first.

What did I feel passionately about? Having been a leader, leadership consultant, coach and speaker for most of my life, I know that I have always been successful in influencing others to become more impactful, confident performers – at work or in life. I love to be the match that ignites others to choose to be at their best. I felt confident that my purpose is to help others recognise their strengths, to become their best self, to be resilient when challenged, to be able to repeat their successes over and over.

This clarity was my pivot and since this time, I have reshaped my life accordingly.

I'd paid one hell of a price but now was the time to make that worthwhile! *Why waste a good accident?!*

It was the best feeling to come to that realisation and I have never felt happier and more fulfilled than I am now, helping others realise their potential. I hope my story can inspire you, that in some way, big or small, I can help you find a way to feel confident in your choices, to know where you are strong and to recognise how valuable you are.

Identifying my purpose, set my direction. I continued studying positive psychology. I was fascinated by what I was learning and the more I learned about how we can change our lives for better by rethinking how we think, the more I practised strategies and played out different psychologist's theories and recommendations. Let's be quite frank, I've had more opportunities to try out all of these than most people! And what I discovered was that we have so much power in us, to live our lives as we aspire to but fear (of change, of failure, of uncertainty...just to name a few) and a lack of understanding, can hold us back from achieving our potential and prevent us from creating the optimal conditions to thrive. When I became a Gallup® Strengths coach everything solidified.

My purpose has given me the reason to keep going, the tenacity to get back up each time I'm knocked down. A psychological buffer against every hurdle, it is like an invisible rope that I always have to hand and that I cling on to when I feel I'm losing my direction, or unable to see my path ahead. When I have dark days, I just hold tight and put one foot in front of the other and trust that I will get back on track. Sometimes I need to hold tighter, for longer, but it has never let me down.

As the actress Nanea Hoffman said: *"The opposite of negativity isn't positivity, it's purpose. We don't always feel positive because we aren't meant to but seeking that which gives your purpose – that will sustain you, even when the light is dim and you feel lost. You will find your way again"*

I've learned that when you understand your purpose, it serves as a point of reference for all your actions and decisions, your life stops being an experiment, or an automated habit and, instead, you live with the assurance and conviction that your life has meaning and direction. I'm not only passionate about what I do but now my goals are aligned with the things that excite me. And I know for certain, that every time I feel despondent, in pain, or face a significant crisis, I think of my purpose, deliberately lean on my strengths and I can pull myself back up.

Finding You

"The heart of human excellence often begins to beat when you discover a pursuit that absorbs you, frees you, challenges you, or gives you a sense of meaning, joy, or passion". Terry Orlick

Some people know exactly what they are born to do and where they are headed in life. And then there's the rest of us.

My son, George, was lucky enough to identify his calling in life, at 5 years old. He knew then that he would be a pilot and that anything which connects and helps develop fellow aviators, was his reason for being. With passion and dedication, he is realising his purpose and grasping every opportunity to make incredible things happen. He's not yet 21 years old. I am in awe.

Like him, you may be totally clear on what drives your motivation and meaning in life but I have found that most people haven't discovered this yet and the arrival of COVID-19, bringing with it challenges that we never imagined, has highlighted just how many people are searching for the right focus in their lives. When things are going well, we tend to cruise through our days and become complacent but when circumstances become disruptive and uncertain, then we start to question our motives and priorities. In my coaching capacity as a Gallup® CliftonStrengths® coach, I have, in recent months, during lockdown and remote working, seen key themes emerge - lack of confidence in career and life choices, re-examining decision making, loss of motivation... of control...of efficiency. All of these have manifested in stress, anxiety and confusion. A common factor has been the recognition that many of my clients have lost touch with their *why*; are out of alignment with their unique purpose.

Have you felt restless? Do you think you're missing something but you can't put your finger on what exactly? That you haven't a clear focus? The feeling that your life and /or your career is not as fulfilling as you hoped it could be at this point? Deliberating what it is that you actually *want* to do? That your goals are conflicting and that you're missing balance? Maybe you've done everything right – worked hard at school, put in the hard graft at work and have a great job but you don't feel a strong sense of accomplishment; you yearn to achieve something that is intrinsically *you*.

If you've had any of these nagging feelings, don't ignore them. Please ask yourself *why?* What is holding you back?

With the current global disruptions challenging our status quo and impacting our lives in ways we never anticipated, knowing your purpose is essential to help you stay motivated, feel passionate about what you do and enable you find the courage to reposition your life and advance with long term impact.

Throughout our lives we fit into different roles with different responsibilities. We tend to define ourselves by what we do for a living but that doesn't necessarily mean that it truly reflects who we are and our worth. We all want to reach our potential and feel our life has meaning. Given the hours we spend in generating an income, wearing different hats and spreading ourselves thin, it is important that you follow a path that aligns with YOUR beliefs and principles. We all yearn to create the right balance in our lives, you need to feel you are on course with what matters to you most.

We are encouraged to pass the exams, to follow a traditional path of pursuing steady, safe career options, often looking to achieve professional excellence before we've had time to consider if this plays to our strengths and our passions. If you don't know where to aim your talent, never found your purpose, lost sight of it, or fallen short of it, don't despair. It's never too late to reinvent yourself. Now is a really good time to refocus your energies, give your life meaning and direction and see the new opportunities in front of you.

Numerous studies prove that people with a clear purpose live longer and healthier lives. They cope better with adversity and feel more inspired by all the things they do. If you search, you will find a vast amount of information on why *purpose* matters and all the benefits attached. There is less information to help you start figuring it out. Here's where I want to help you get started. I recommend that when it comes to defining your purpose, that you review Simon Sinek's *Start with WHY* and *Find your WHY*. Another good read is *Ikigai: The Japanese Secret to a Long and Happy Life* by Héctor García.

Getting clear on your purpose

There is no shortcut to identifying your purpose – it's not a quick exercise. Neither is there just one route to discover it. It's a reflective journey that requires you to do a self- audit, to become more self-aware and discover what matters most to you. It takes time and the amount of time varies from person to person. Mostly we are so busy going about our daily lives that we don't take time to figure out who we truly are and what we want. Give yourself that opportunity now. Be sure you are living a life that plays to your strengths and aligns with your values and your passion.

You are certainly not required to have suffered a life altering incident to find your purpose but you will have been through experiences, relationships and transitions of your own, that frame your lens of the world and highlight what matters most to you. That lens can be refocused at any time to see your world differently, so you can discover who you are when you are at your best.

Please grab a pen and paper so you can capture your thoughts and identify opportunities for yourself and when you're ready, I'd like to draw your attention to 3 areas of focus:

1. Get to know yourself

We all think we know ourselves but psychological studies strongly suggest otherwise!

As I explain in the section: ***Leaning on your Strengths***, we all have a natural toolkit of talents which instinctively and intuitively define our thoughts and feelings and influence our behaviours, activities and relationships. Understanding your unique combination, enables you to decide how best to apply your talents to help you achieve the things you want to accomplish. In other words, when you know your *purpose,* you then can focus your talents and invest in them appropriately (increased knowledge, skills and practice) so that they become your absolute go-to resources for taking specific actions towards achieving your goals. The more you understand how to leverage them, the stronger those resources become and the greater your ability to do things exceptionally well. As Gallup® points out: **Talent x Investment = Strength**

Let's start focusing your awareness on you with the following questions:

- What are the critical things I have to do?

- What's working well?

- What are the challenges I face?

- What change would I like to bring about?

- When I am working at my best what does that look/feel like? (*think about your successes, what did you do to be successful?*)

- What makes me come alive?

- What depletes me? Irritates me? Bores me?

- What values matter to me?

- Where do I create impact?

- What do I want to be known for?

The more I focused my attention on what I do well, I began to see how my strengths supported me in achieving my successes – and where they got in my way and how I reacted; recognising the importance of my values and the frustration I feel if they are ignored or crossed. By consciously noticing the connections, I have learned how to leverage my opportunities even more, so that my strengths are aligned with my purpose.

2. Determine your purpose

If your passion does not align with your purpose, it becomes difficult to motivate yourself towards a goal.

Based on the Western interpretation of the Japanese Ikigai, I find this simple framework below, helpful for determining your purpose as it enables you start to single out your passion and how to connect that with practical mediums through which to express it.

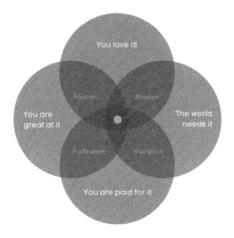

A simplified interpretation of the Japanese concept of Ikigai

It encompasses 4 areas:

- what you love

- what you're good at

- what the world needs

- what you can get paid for.

What do you want to accomplish? What issues are close to your heart? What do you feel most strongly about? What do you want to take a stand for? What legacy do you want to leave?

What are you identifying here, about yourself?

Use your responses to look at the overlaps of the various circles and ask yourself some new questions, for example: How can I combine what I love to do with what the world needs? How can I combine what I'm good at with things I can get paid for? Look at the complete picture and try to find connections.

By understanding what motivates you and makes you happy, you can gain the courage and understanding to realise which goals you should pursue and what you should be saying no to.

Even though I knew what mattered to me most and I can explain it in so many ways, it still took me considerable thought and time to narrow it into one sentence (with Maximiser® as my top CliftonStrengths® theme, I'm a perfectionist and always looking to find a better way to express it! A bigger version!) but here's my bottom line:

To inspire people to recognise their own greatness, so they can do extraordinary things.

3. Measure what matters

People who don't stand for something, can easily fall for anything. Deciding how you want to measure your life means making a stand for something and then living your life in alignment with it. If you fail to identify your purpose, you may end up falling in line with someone else's purpose, in absence of your own. And why on earth would any of us want to live someone else's dream?!

Identify where you are and what you want

- What do you enjoy about your work now; what needs to change?

- Where is you next move?

- What do you want to achieve?

- What is your competitive advantage?

Shift your lens to review what you do

- Are you taking on the right challenges?

- Are you stretching yourself in line with your strengths?

- How often do you find yourself working to FLOW? (your perfect balance between challenge and motivation)

- What would you do differently, if you knew you couldn't fail?

It's important that you spot the difference between what you do versus why you do it. Knowing your purpose may compel you to take on challenges that will stretch you as much as they inspire you. When you amend your current lens of your world, you can profoundly change your experience of it.

As Oprah Winfrey says: "You have to find what sparks a light in you so that you, in your own way, can illuminate the world".

When your life is on track with your purpose and aligns with your personal strengths, you are at your most powerful.

This journey called life will be over before you realise it. Why spend another minute living a life that isn't personally meaningful to you? Recognise your personal power.

Don't live a random existence. Life is too short.

CALL TO ACTION!

"Resilience is knowing that you are the only one that has the power and responsibility to pick yourself up" Mary Holloway

Now, more than ever, as we face a disruptive, uncertain future, it's important you feel confident and prepared; to make smarter choices when you face the challenges and opportunities ahead.

Which part of your life needs a boost?

What do you need to focus on to be at your best and how will you go about making the changes you wish to see?

How I can help you

I have found that most people don't recognise their own greatness and often reach milestones through trial and error. Wouldn't it save so much time and effort, if you knew exactly *which* buttons to push, the self-assurance in knowing where your greatest potential lies, enabling you to focus on the *right* things to accomplish your goals?

Through Gallup® CliftonStrengths®, I enable individuals, teams and organisations to recognise what makes them uniquely powerful and leverage their strengths and resilience, to thrive in today's business.

"No one else is you. And that, right there, is your power". Marcus Buckingham

You have great potential; don't leave your future to chance! Decide what needs to change and change it.

If you'd like to know more about how your strengths will enable you to flourish, or you need some advice on how to move forwards, do reach out to me: laura@lauraeverestconsulting.com

My top 5 CliftonStrengths®: Maximiser ® Achiever® Arranger® Communication® Focus®

ACKNOWLEDGEMENTS

Writing this personal journey has brought together so many different threads of my life, that it would take a whole other book to thank each of you, individually, for your kindness, friendship and support. I am blessed and grateful to you all, my friends.

There are very specific people to whom I am indebted and I'd like to draw particular recognition to.

First and foremost, my extended family – Graham, Lucy, Mum and Dad, without whom our family journey would have been significantly harder and longer. Amanda and Bridgitte Maree-Descoins who have been alongside me every step of the way. Nita and Tinah who have looked after me and our family all these years. I'm so very lucky to have you all!

My closest tribe who are so encouraging of everything I do, have been tremendous friends and are the reason I could get back to work successfully, after each setback – Norman Grimes, Nancy and Matt Clarke, Nicole Samuels, Nigel Bradford, Bev Mileham.

Mr Andrew Goldberg and his amazing team at the Wellington Hospital, London, and Bev Strathearn – you are the reason why I am still upright and active. To say I'm thankful and appreciative sounds ridiculously understated; I am beyond grateful for all you have done and continue to do.

A very special thank you to Phil Bedford for being a great mentor; Zen Khan and all the Asentiv community for your ongoing support.

A specific shout out Scott Wright at Gallup® for his licencing support.

Thank you to everyone at Notion Press for their technical expertise and to the excellent Pixel Roses for such great photographic images.

Richard, George and Anna – I have made it through because of you.

Nothing is impossible.
The word itself says "I'm possible!"

Made in the USA
Coppell, TX
12 July 2021